AESTHETICS AND ARCHITECTURE

Continuum Aesthetics

Series Editor: Derek Matravers (Open University)

Aesthetics and Film, Katherine Thomson
Aesthetics and Literature, David Davies
Aesthetics and Morality, Elisabeth Schellekens
Aesthetics and Music, Andy Hamilton
Aesthetics and Nature, Glenn Parsons
Aesthetics and Painting, Jason Gaiger

of the Bank of England as celestial homes of the gods; and in our appreciation of such parts of architecture, we understand the allusion to our classical past. These cases of representation, however, are not central cases of architectural work. They are marginal just because they disguise their architectural purpose in feigning to be architectural works belonging to a grander tradition. They are, we might suppose, the architectural equivalent of *trompe l'oeil*; and *trompe l'oeil* might be thought as central to our understanding of representational painting as the folly and the ædicule are to architecture.[3] That is to say that when we look at a folly or an ædicule, while we perceive the building at which we look, say a gardener's shed, we nevertheless have an experience *as of* the represented building, a classical temple. Is this compatible with the claims of the classicist? Is this our common grasp of representation, taken broadly; and is this the way we think we should take primary cases of architectural understanding?

A spectator who could not see the face of another in the portrait at which she looks, would have failed to understand the painting. A spectator who fails to see that a sculpture of a horse *is of a horse* would have failed to understand the sculpture. It does not follow that a spectator who fails to see the primitive building in the classical building will have failed in his understanding of the building. For, the building is not 'of' anything. (Imagine the following thought: 'I can see that it is a building, but: I cannot see *of what* it is a building'. That thought is out of place in our assessment of architectural works. It displays the wrong kind of response to architecture.) Further, an architect could construct a classical building, in accordance with the traditional constraints imposed by the classical orders, and yet he could still fail to see the primitive building in his classical design. This would entail the following possibility: that an architect could design a building, create a work of architecture, and yet utterly fail to understand the building he has thus produced. If it is an open question as to whether or not classical buildings, properly understood, are representational, then the activity of designing these buildings cannot properly have representation as part of its intention. If it cannot have representation as part of its intention, then either buildings are representational independently of the intentions of those who design them or they are not representational (since this cannot properly be an intention of the architect). Representation is an intentional activity. The face that I see in the clouds is not a representation. The face that I see in a portrait is. The difference between the face in the painting and the face in the clouds is that the former is the result of an artist's intention; while the latter is not. Since representation is an intentional activity, it cannot be that buildings are, in any fully fledged sense, representational.

II

In order to put these loose thoughts on a more secure footing, we need to say something about what it is for architecture to be a *visual* art. After all, representation cuts across both the visual and the non-visual arts. The novel and the poem are both capable of representing the world and in ways that reveal to us important features of it. But while they are representational arts, they are not visual arts. Painting and sculpture are visual arts. It is an important feature of our appreciation of them that we include in our account of them something of their visual character.

It is a feature of the arts in general that they provide us with experiences we value. In order to demonstrate this we need to consider the nature of experience. Experiences are subjective. That is to say that for any experience there must be a subject of that experience. There is something it is like to have an experience. It has a 'feel', so to speak. Ordinarily speaking, experiences are given to their subjects via some mode of perception. We see things, hear things, feel things, smell things and taste things. There is something it is like to see something, hear something, smell something or taste something. And what it is like to have an experience can be either pleasant or unpleasant.

Contrast this feature of mental life with belief. There are many beliefs that I have of which I remain unaware for most of my waking life. And for most of my beliefs it is true that I remain unaware of them in my sleeping life. For instance, that my mother and father were married is a belief I hold; but it is a belief that rarely intrudes upon my awareness. The vast majority of my beliefs remain beyond my consciousness and its contents. That is to say that there is nothing it is like to have a belief. Beliefs, unlike experiences, do not have a 'feel' that is present to consciousness. We shall discuss this further in Chapter 10.

Of a piece with this account of our mental life, we see that experience has a precise duration, while the holding of a belief does not. Experience is always present to consciousness, while belief is not. Experience is always in the presence of an object, where 'object' is to be construed broadly. My attention is directed, as it were, at the object of experience. Now for some objects of experience, the object might be an object of thought and not of perception. This is going to be true for most poetry and most novels, where the reader directs his attention toward the thought contained in the rhythmic unfolding of the poem, for instance. He can rehearse the poem in his head without requiring that it is read to him or that he himself has a copy in front of him in order that he might read it. The point is that his consciousness is consumed with the thought that the poem presents to him; and that he is, in an important sense, in the presence of the poem while he undergoes an experience of it.

For some arts, however, the mode of perception plays an important part in the experience we have of the work. Representational painting, for instance, requires that we attend to the surface of a paint-smeared canvas in order to have an experience of the represented object as we look at that canvas. The work of music requires our attention to the sounds as they unfold in sequence, so that we can experience the music contained in those sounds. Painting is therefore a visual art; and music is an acoustic art. For literature, there is no fixed location wherein the work resides. It is problematic, to say the least, to locate the work of art which constitutes each piece of music. For the visual arts, however, we seem to have a less troublesome time. The experiences we have of works of visual art reside in the perceptions we undergo in front of the works themselves. That is not to say that questions do not arise for some works of visual art. It is merely to claim that for a large range of cases, the perception of the work forms the substratum for a further experience. In drawing together these thoughts, we can say that the experience of all works of art is in the presence of the work. However, for different kinds of works of art, that presence will be differently identified and realized. For works of visual art, the presence is to be identified with an object of visual perception. In seeing the object, the work of art, we are afforded an experience. That experience adheres to the perception, so to speak. This is a phenomenological description of what it is to look at a piece of visual art. Architecture is a visual art and requires a description of our experience of it in terms that render its appearance intelligible to us. Contrast this, for instance, with our appreciation of the novel.

Nevertheless, in arguing that our understanding is delimited by a requirement to reside in the experience, it is important not to isolate the work of architecture from its tradition or from other works of architecture beyond the confines of the tradition. It is a requirement, then, that our understanding of the work of architecture describes our experience and at the same time connects it with our acquaintance with the tradition and with our knowledge of other traditions or styles. If this is so then we need to make clear that in referring to the tradition we are not venturing further than the limits of experience. That is, the spectator's experience must contain, or must be internally connected with, other experiences he has had of other buildings. It is not that other buildings are represented in his experience, but rather that other buildings and his acquaintance with them provide his present experience with at least something of its character.

A dramatic example of such a case might illustrate this point. Let us suppose that A and B are listening to Vaughan Williams' *Variations on a Theme by Thomas Tallis*. Further, we might suppose, that A is well acquainted with Tallis's work but that B has never heard any English Renaissance music before. Then A's experience will be qualitatively different from B's. Both A and B respond to the work *as music*. Here, A's response, his experience of the work, is coloured by its *internal connection* with the work of Tallis. Of course, B will make other connections, perhaps with other works of Vaughan Williams, or with other works by Vaughan Williams's contemporaries; but these responses will be more or less fleshed out by the descriptions of them that each is able to bring to bear; or, perhaps more importantly, by the descriptions of the music to which each feels able to assent. (This last clause allows each to be able to have an experience without necessarily being able to produce a description of it.) Nothing further to, or outside of, the experience has been invoked to explain the difference in their understanding of the piece of music to which each has listened.

So, when a spectator is standing in the cloister of Borromini's San Carlo alle Quattro Fontane, his experience of that building will be more or less rich depending on his familiarity with the history of architecture pertinent to the building in which he now stands. Provided that he is acquainted with the classical orders and the strictness demanded in their application, he shall see Borromini's cloister as impertinent, audacious or even outrageous. These descriptions will capture his experience given that the experience is so coloured by his other experiences. They will explain his amusement at the building, or his sneaking admiration, or his utter disgust. In explaining why he so sees the building he will call upon another to share the experience he is undergoing, and to share his response to it. That response to the building is contained in his experience of it and so he will not have ventured beyond the experience in providing an account of his appreciative understanding.

What the representational theorist takes for the representational relation in this particular instance is, perhaps, better conceived as a connection between works of art generally, so that in experiencing one work, the spectator's experience of other works impinges upon his present experience. This point can be fleshed out by looking at Wittgenstein's work on aspect seeing. When a figure is seen as having a certain aspectual *content*, that representational content is projected onto it.

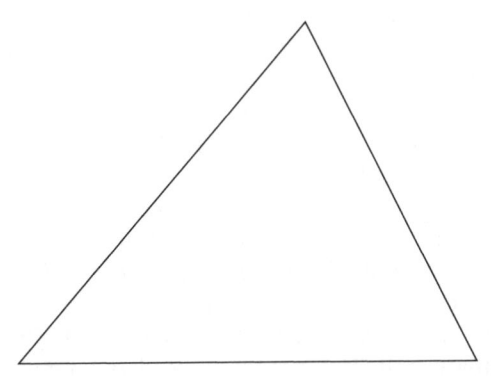

Seeing the triangle now as an arrowhead pointing to the left, now as a solid plane with a triangular void cut into it, now as a pyramid; and so on, we see the figure and bring it under observational descriptions which are constitutive of the different experiences afforded by each such description. In each case we project content onto the perception, thereby treating the figure as if it is *of* the content we project. Rather as we do when we notice the content of a picture.

A related but distinct phenomenon, is when I notice the resemblance between two faces. In the case where only one face is present to me, I nevertheless notice a relation between the two faces I have in mind. However, the face that is present does not have the face it is seen as resembling as content. The face present to me does not have content. Nevertheless I can see the resemblance between this face and another. As Wittgenstein has it:

> And it is not so much as if I were comparing the object with a picture set beside it, but as if the object *coincided* with the picture. So I see only one thing, not two.[4]

One might say: 'What I saw was memory laden.'[5]

The previous case, where I look at a figure, say the triangle, and project *content* onto it, is structurally similar to the representational relation. It is as if the triangle is provided with content.

Now, when we look at buildings and see them as related to other buildings, it is more like the case of noticing a resemblance than recognizing the content – recognizing what the building 'is of'. So, while buildings might call to mind other buildings, they do not thereby have other buildings as their representational content.

If our reflections upon classicism so far have seemed negative, it is only because we have been assessing the philosophical dimension of the theory that has been invoked to establish and sustain it. That is not to say that works of classical architecture are not among the most beautiful works in the world. Rather, it is to deny the very broad claims that would have placed classicism at the heart of architecture, with other forms of building either excluded from the domain altogether; or left to claim whatever derivative status they can. (Some forms of modernism have been designed in accordance with certain dominant classicist characteristics. Some, for instance, see 'stripped classicism' as such a form of modernism.)[6]

How then are we to account for those classical buildings that we think are beautiful works of architecture? Here we might look at individual buildings and begin to describe them in critical terms. The buildings are modest (as opposed to overblown), they are delicate (as opposed to heavy or dull), they are well situated (as opposed to plonked in the landscape), they execute the orders with charm (as opposed to being slavishly obedient) and so on. That is to say that within the terms of classicism, we can discriminate between those that are fine examples and those that are merely ordinary. The fine examples will be buildings that fit well under our conception of architecture when we eventually arrive at such a point.

We can now begin to see how an understanding of a work of architecture brings with it an evaluation that is characteristic of our appreciation of works of art generally. To understand a building is to see it in a certain way. It is to be disposed to give such and such descriptions which articulate the experiences that we have in its presence. Such understanding can be clumsy, rudimentary, subtle or deep. And it can vary in degrees according to how much attention we pay to the building under scrutiny. However, this admission of degrees of understanding can easily be accommodated within the context of a wider aesthetic theory which places emphasis upon the *experience* of the spectator.

CHAPTER 2

MODERNISM

Enlightenment philosophy emerged during the seventeenth and eighteenth centuries; when scholarship replaced worship – the light of reason thereby replacing the light of heaven. Thus we find that a conception of what (or who) we are develops in the philosophy of the modern period. The rise of science, as the fundamental basis of our knowledge and understanding of the world, has its inception in the work of the Enlightenment philosophers. Arguably, these philosophers turned philosophical attention away from metaphysics and instead directed it toward epistemology. The rationalists – Descartes, Leibniz and Spinoza on the Continent – sought to secure our knowledge on the basis of reflection alone. On the other hand, the empiricists – Locke, Berkeley and Hume in Great Britain – believed that observation was the only reliable source of human knowledge.

Perhaps the greatest philosopher of the Enlightenment is Immanuel Kant. It was Kant's three critiques that aimed to provide us with a full account of our rationality. In this venture he set limits to the nature of reason as that can be applied within three distinct domains: the theoretical, the ethical and the aesthetic. In the first of these works, *The Critique of Pure Reason*, he attempted to place limits on the use of theoretical reason and thereby circumscribe the realm of rational belief; with its attendant constraints on what can be known. Thus, he sought to explain the relationship between mind and world; and in so doing he found it necessary to provide an account of the 'manifold of perception'.

Roughly speaking, our sensory input is filtered through a conceptual framework, the result of which is that we see trees on hills beyond and above us (for instance). That is to say that our perception is governed by a mechanism which fits sensations into patterns of pre-established concepts. It is the work of the imagination to capture fleeting sensations that would be otherwise unruly; and to impose its order upon them, thereby processing them into regulated perceptions. What perception provides us with is access to a conceptually structured world.

Whatever one might want to say about the arguments to be found in the first of the critiques, it is with the second and third that we might be most interested in getting to grips with modernism and its implications for the humanities. We shall return to Kant's use of imagination when we consider modernist aesthetics below. That science emerged during the Enlightenment as the authority to which all rational thought must defer, is challenged by Kant's second and third critiques. For Kant regards both ethics and aesthetics as properly governed by reason and the judgements at which each arrives is available only to the rational mind.

In *The Critique of Practical Reason*, the authority of the church was replaced by the authority of reason. Obedience to the commandments of God is no longer the method by which we must regiment the practical aspects of our lives. How then must they be lived? In the absence of divine authority, it has seemed to some that morality is a matter of choice; and that living a full life is a matter of maximizing lifestyle choices. (It is small wonder that those cultures obedient to their clerical teachers and to the wisdom of their ancients should consider western liberalism as decadent and degenerate.) At least, as it stands, morality becomes a matter of subjective 'feel'; a matter of finding our actions and those of others comfortable. Kant, however, was determined to give an account that would not merely dispense with the authority of religion, but that would also replace that authority. He sought, that is, to provide us with a *rational basis* upon which to act. In the second critique, Kant replaces the commandments of God with the commandment of reason – the 'categorical imperative'.

Since we have identified two ethical theories emerging from the Enlightenment, it might be illuminating to mention contractualism before returning to Kant's ethical theory. It is worth so doing because contractualism is of a piece with a dominant strain of ethical thinking within western liberalism; and that strain might be thought of as the default position within our western culture. In rehearsing ethical theories at this juncture, we shall be able to consider architecture as a public art in Chapter 9. It is in virtue of the place that ethical thinking has in modernist thought that we can come to see the relationship between ethical and aesthetic judgements.

The view is, arguably, a sceptical view which offers morality up to politics, itself a pragmatist means of regulating behaviour between agents within a community. The contractualist claims that, since there are no predetermined laws of behaviour that we are required to obey, we must regulate behaviour by means of a contract between members of the community. Agents within a community are simply entered into an agreement to behave toward each other in ways which offer mutual benefit. Jean-Jacques Rousseau's *The Social Contract* was published in 1762, a quarter of a century before its effects were to be felt in his native France. It was to find a strong adherent in the twentieth century in the American philosopher John Rawls. According to contractualists, we are entered into a contractual agreement with others; and this agreement, which can vary over time in accordance with changes in law, binds all members of the community in whose law the contract is enshrined. It is not that I freely enter into a contract. Rather, the system of morality into which I am entered, is of mutual benefit to all members of the community. (The system is a good system if it is the kind of system that I would willingly agree to enter, independently of my present self-interests.) In arguing for such a contractualist position, we are to remember that there is nothing in the world that makes something *intrinsically* right or wrong. Rather, we look to mutual benefits and deem patterns of action good or bad according to whether they, in principle, promote benefits to members of the community. Investment in mutual benefit is not in and of itself an ethical recommendation. It is merely prudent. Thus contractualism is seen as explaining our moral intuitions in non-moral terms. Contractualism, that is, explains morality away. That is why it must be considered a sceptical account of morality. We act 'morally' just because it is mutually advantageous to do so.

Contractualism has its counterpart in aesthetics. In matters of art, perhaps more than anywhere else in human affairs, concession is immediately given to those who argue that values are radically culturally relative. In effect, the view is that there is no constraint upon how we are to judge works of art. All that we have is a collection of likes and dislikes. These likes form a weight of 'judgement'; and this judgement determines value in the marketplace. But there is nothing independent to which we can make appeal in coming to an aesthetic judgement. Like contractualism, the view is ultimately sceptical; in that it merely records the accumulation of likes without further comment. It makes no ultimate claim to confirm or deny any judgement. Again, one thinks of those cultures whose conception of art is shaped by the clerics or political masters; and one sees in their perspective upon western contemporary art and architecture how shallow our decadent attitude to our cultural environment has become. In matters of morality and art, values, on the contractualist model, are merely negotiated.

AESTHETICS AND ARCHITECTURE

By contrast the political art of the Marxist or fascist state, or the religious art of the Christian, Jewish or Islamic world, are given foundation in a philosophically realist position. I do not mean to underwrite any of these realist positions. However, I do want to emphasize that radical anti-realism with respect to ethics and aesthetics leads to a view of art and architecture that ultimately has to relinquish its claim to value.

Kant is no such sceptic. In rehearsing the nature of practical reason he develops a notion of the person and derives from that notion a conception of what is required of moral agency. Since the combined purpose of the three critiques is to provide a full account of our rational nature, it is to reason that Kant turns in developing his conception of the moral agent. We have an idea of what it is for an organism to flourish. We know, that is, what it is for organisms to be healthy specimens of their particular species. Human beings, however, can flourish under two separate descriptions. A person can flourish as a healthy specimen of his species, as when we look upon the young athletic competitors at the Olympic Games. We know what it is for the cellular structure of a human being to be in good shape. However, rational agents flourish when they enter into rational projects. It might well be that an agent's cellular structure is degenerate according to his advanced years; and yet he might still flourish as a rational agent in pursuit of rational ends. Thus, someone who has passed his finest days as a healthy organism might yet flourish as a rational being, pursuing research, composing symphonies, reading novels or tending to his back garden. Indeed, he might only reflect bitterly upon the nature of life in order to flourish as a rational agent. So, it seems that we have two notions of flourishing that can be applied to human beings, the one in light of their nature as organisms; the other in light of their nature as rational agents. It is to the latter that Kant directs his attention when considering the nature of practical reason.

If a course of action is recommended to someone as an efficient means of achieving some end an agent has in mind, then that recommendation is an injunction for him to act accordingly. So, if someone were to want to be in Brighton for 17:00 and the quickest and cheapest available means of getting there is by taking the 15:45 train from London Victoria, then taking that train is a course of action recommended to him. If he wants x then y is the course of action he should pursue. However, should he not have the specified want, the recommendation no longer has its authority. The command, 'Take the 15:45' is to be obeyed only by those whose desires shall be satisfied by the results of such actions; their timely arrival at Brighton. Such is the stature of the hypothetical imperative. It recommends courses of action relative to an agent's wants. It supplies the means, given that an agent has some end in mind. However, it says nothing about those ends and passes no judgement upon them.

The categorical imperative, by contrast, recommends courses of action that must be taken independently of an agent's wants. When an agent looks upon the world with the moral gaze, he is to consider what he there encounters as if seen and considered by any other rational being. That is to say that he must hold his own interests in abeyance. In considering the practicalities of life he is called upon to see himself and others alike as belonging to a kingdom of ends – a world in which all rational agents enjoy the same respect. In making moral choices, the agent is to see himself as disposed to act in ways which must be recommended not just for him in this situation, but for any rational being who finds himself confronted with these circumstances. Thus Kant derived the categorical imperative: 'Act always on that maxim that you could will as a universal law'. The recommendation to act in accordance with this injunction is not relativized, as was the case with the hypothetical imperative. It states, for all rational agents, that this is how each must act when confronted by some moral circumstance in which there is a need to take action.

It is not difficult to understand the appeal of this account of morality, especially in light of the rise of science and the centrality of humanity in the new scheme of things. Reason is now placed upon the throne of authority. Enthroned reason alone is set above us constraining our choice of action; demanding of each that we act this way rather than that. Moreover, these 'recommendations to act' bear the mark of objectivity, since reason stands outside of any subjective consideration an agent might have that derives from his personal interests. It is as a rational agent that he is enjoined to act. It is because he belongs to a world in which reason permits him to rise above his nature as an organism, that he is constrained to act in a certain way. It is in the ability to act according to the constraint of reason that he finds his freedom. Indeed, such a view provides an instant explanation of why it is that discrimination against human beings in terms of race, gender, sexuality and disability are intrinsically wrong. If we are to consider another in terms of his race, gender, sexuality or disability, we are bringing into consideration features of his empirical nature that lie outside his rationality. We would be treating him not as a rational agent but as an organism. It is in consideration of his rationality alone that we find ourselves accommodated with him in a kingdom of equals, each with an obligation to respect the other. The categorical imperative claims universal acceptance. This is how an agent feels moved to act; and this is how any other rational agent should feel moved to act. And what would move him and any other rational agent is reason alone.

Universal claims need not be met to have the structural feature of universality written into them. The point about the claim is not whether it is met; rather, it is about the strength of the claim's ambition. Whether or not we comply with the claim, it demands universal acceptance. We shall meet this kind of claim again when considering aesthetic judgements.

This has been a rudimentary sketch of the structure of the thought of one of the greatest philosophers of the West. Nevertheless, I hope to have said enough to have brought us to a point where we can consider aesthetics and see how the shape of aesthetics in Kant's thought is important to understand modernism in the history of art and architecture.

The first and second critiques are concerned with the regulation of our beliefs and our actions respectively; the third with the regulation of a peculiar kind of experience. That is to say that each of the critiques provides an account of how reason legitimates certain characteristics of our mental life. The rationalists and empiricists had brought epistemology to the forefront of philosophical discourse. Kant, in attempting to resolve the tensions between the two strands of modern philosophical thought, continued to place epistemology at the heart of his philosophy. Thus science was given a sure footing; its methodology underwritten by the broader rational structure of philosophical enquiry.

However, his thought on practical and aesthetic reason extended his view of the human mind beyond the realm of knowledge and brought it to focus on action and experience. We have had a brief look at his practical philosophy. It is with his work on aesthetics that we now turn. I have said that Kant sought to provide an account of the *rational* regulation of a peculiar kind of experience. That might at first seem odd. Certainly, the empiricists, who thought of the mind as a *tabula rasa*, would have had difficulty with such a view. For the empiricist the mind is a passive receptor of information; impressionable in its witness of external events. The world, as it were, imposes itself upon the mind by invading the perceptual apparatus; thereby leaving its mark in experience. Our knowledge, according to the empiricists, is written across the previously blank slate of the mind.

What place has reason in such a causal account of knowledge and experience?

In *The Critique of Judgement*, however, Kant was not concerned with knowledge gained through experience – *a posteriori* knowledge. He had dealt with this in the first critique. (And we have, in summary, outlined the structure of his thought on empirical knowledge above.) In the third critique, Kant is concerned with experience that is set aside from the acquisition of knowledge. His concern is with the apprehension of the beautiful – with aesthetic experience. While imagination had a crucial role to play in 'the manifold of perception', it is recruited to a different task in our apprehension of beauty. In our judging something beautiful, Kant thinks, we disengage the imagination from the task it undertakes in the machinery by which we acquire knowledge through perception. In the free play of imagination, we are allowed to look at the world independently of any governing concepts.

If we look at the world as if it bears the imprint of design, but without concerning ourselves with the specific nature of design, we shall employ the imagination without engaging the cognitive faculty. That is, the imagination is no longer employed to furnish us with knowledge of the world. And so, for Kant, while aesthetics engages the machinery of perception, and hence of knowledge, it is not concerned with the *acquisition* of knowledge. It might be thought, therefore, that our aesthetic responses to the world are thereby rendered unruly and ungovernable. Kant, in the third critique, sought to overcome this suggestion.

The importance of the third critique lies in the place it sets out for aesthetics in the description of what constitutes the human mind; and in the significance it establishes for aesthetics within human affairs. Kant is rightly concerned with giving an account of how it is that we can make judgements that are at once subjective and universal. That is to say judgements of beauty are held to be pleasing to the subject, who recognizes in his judgement that his claim demands universal assent. The pleasure he feels is a pleasure containing within itself a recommendation to all such constituted minds. Since it is not the object's purpose that enters our aesthetic apprehension, it is the form of the object alone to which we respond. And in this response we recognize that others, too, must so respond. The pure beauty, of which Kant writes, is best conceived as natural beauty. (Although he does, at one point, seem to ascribe pure beauty to musical form.)[1] Our concern, once we have set out the intellectual framework within which to focus upon the aesthetics of architecture, is with dependent or accessory or fixed beauty.

AESTHETICS AND ARCHITECTURE

Section 16 of the third critique opens with the following paragraph:

> There are two kinds of beauty, free beauty (*pulchritude vaga*) and merely accessory beauty (*pulchritude adhaerens*). Free beauty does not presuppose a concept of what the object is [meant] to be. Accessory beauty does presuppose such a concept, as well as the object's perfection in terms of that concept. The free kinds of beauty are called (self-subsistent) beauties of this or that thing. The other kind of beauty is accessory to a concept (i.e., it is conditioned beauty) and as such is attributed to objects that fall under the concept of a particular purpose.

In dealing with the fine arts, Kant aligns each with what he variously calls accessory, dependent or fixed beauty. Painting and sculpture (as well as architecture) are fixed beauties. And so it is not just because architecture serves our human purposes that we bring it under the conception of fixed beauty. Painting is a fixed beauty because when considering the beauty of its instances, we are to regard the object of our attention as a painting; and not merely as a formal arrangement of lines and shapes across a flat surface. For Kant, of course, painting was a *representational* medium. And so looking at paintings meant looking at pictures. And so, I believe, Kant thought that the perfectibility of a painting was to be, at least in part, connected with the nature of a perfect picture of some object, person or scene. (It is, perhaps, a strange irony that it is Kant who so strongly influenced Clement Greenberg; the latter going on to inform and promote abstract painting in the 1950s.) Paintings, then, are beautiful objects that depict objects, persons or scenes. Architecture consists in the making of beautiful buildings, each brought into the world to serve our purposes. Paintings, however, are beautiful in virtue of bringing about representational imagery.

A beautiful book, as an object, might contain humdrum information or even a very poor quality novel. The content of the book and its formal properties *as a physical object* seem to be separable, not only in thought, but in substance too. How is this possible; and what can we learn from it? The identity of works of art are prescribed by what it is for something to be an instantiation of it. Picasso's *Desmoiselles d'Avignon* is identical with that painted canvas stretched over a wooden frame and hanging in the San Francisco Museum of Modern Art. To set fire to and destroy that painted canvas is to set fire to and destroy *Desmoiselles d'Avignon*. A poem, however, is not identical with any (or all) printed inscriptions of it. I might easily throw into the incinerator a battered copy of a poem I have hitherto kept in my pocket, having typed out a fresher version.

Kant's Prayer

> God to whom my life is owed,
> Not life I thank you for, nor love,
> But two great gifts that you bestowed:
> The law within, the stars above.[2]

The verse 'Kant's Prayer' is inscribed above. However, even if every inscription of it were destroyed, provided that someone remembered the poem by heart, it could be re-inscribed, or even rehearsed at a reading. That is to say that the nature of the physical instantiation of the poem, whether that be a printed inscription or its delivery at a reading, is relatively independent of the aesthetic properties of the poem *as a poem*. Of course, the physical instantiation might have aesthetic properties as an example of an instantiation. That is to say, the poem can be beautifully presented in calligraphy on parchment paper, but the poem will be no better *as a poem* for all that.

So too with the book. The book might be a beautiful object *as a designed physical object*; but this aesthetic character remains relatively free from considerations of the content of the book. Two books might look, as objects, fairly similar in respect to their aesthetic character. However, their content, and hence their status as novels might differ considerably. I might, for instance, be unable to distinguish, on the basis of the aesthetic character of the book as an object, between a novel consisting of unremarkable trashy pornography by some journeyman writer of such a pulp-fiction genre, from a great work by Jean-Paul Sartre, for example, *The Age of Reason*. The form of the novel, as with the form of the poem, does not consist in its appearance as a visual object.

To say of the book that, as an object, it is a beautiful thing, does not require any consideration of its content. For these purposes we might think that the sketchbook or the notebook are the best examples to focus our attention upon. In sketching or writing in the formerly blank book, we do not alter its aesthetic characteristics *as an object*.

It is with this in mind that we looked at Picasso's *Desmoiselles d'Avignon*. The form of that painting is not independent of how the painting looks. Indeed, to the contrary, it is in virtue of how the painting looks that we are able to *see* the form that is the vehicle for the content. That the painting is beautiful, *as a painting*, requires the attribution of beauty to the object *as a depiction*. In this important sense, painting is a visual art. We can read poems and novels by looking at the printed page. But we can also have them read to us; or we can feel them on the page if we are trained in Braille. The visuality of a printed poem is not (standardly) part of its aesthetic character *as a poem*. Since painting is a visual art, its visual appearance is *essential* to it as a work of art.

It is a feature of modernism within the arts that each art has begun to turn its attention to the means by which it is constructed. Painting turned to abstract colour and pattern; sculpture to line, plane and volume; music to sound; poetry to words and, in some cases, typology. That might seem odd at first reading. But the arts deliberately sought to emphasize the stuff from which each was made as the primary source of our interest in the particular art. Thus, we see that formalism spread itself across the arts. I do not want to delve into the notion of formalism in the other arts too deeply. Suffice it to say that the representational arts turned away from naturalism in order to foreground the formal aspects of the work under consideration; while the abstract arts, such as music, turned away from tone, melody and harmony, in order to prioritize our interest in sound alone.

But what is the stuff of architecture and what were the properties upon which it could focus attention? Independently of any consideration of function, the architect could attend to materials from which the work was built – and in particular he could celebrate the new materials being manufactured in industry. Thus he would be able to attend to structures made of steel, glass and concrete in terms of planes, voids, volumes and spaces. An abstract conception of these elements could render modern buildings as complex compositions independent of any supposed use. Here we might think of Mies van der Rohe's Barcelona Pavilion, a beautiful jewel of a modernist building fit for no purpose whatsoever. (It is surely too draughty, even for the mild Mediterranean winter; and it is utterly defenceless against the constant stream of cheap-airline tourists through the long hot summer.)

One strong tendency within modernism in painting is abstract expressionism. That movement was supported by the art historian Clement Greenberg, who gave to the movement its strongest and clearest espousal in his 'Modernist Painting'.[3] Influenced by his peculiar reading of Kant, Greenberg sought to free painting of its

3 Mies van der Rohe: Barcelona Pavilion

superfluous task of representation; thereby liberating the medium to focus upon its pure form. As such, Greenberg sought an aesthetic that was free from content and would be an example of Kantian 'free beauty'. As such, the art work established itself as a locus of beauty, as opposed to a bearer of meaning. It is unclear whether any of the painters supported and promoted by him subscribed to his spare and abstract version of aesthetics. Nevertheless, in Greenberg's theory we have the starkest expression of one version of the aesthetics of modernism. It might be unfair to cite Mies van der Rohe's Barcelona Pavilion as an architectural counterpart to such formalism, but it is clear that the pavilion is not to be seen as a functionalist piece of modernism. And it is also clear that the form of that building is at the heart of our understanding of the architect's project. We shall return to the notion of meaning in architecture in Part II.

Modernism in the other arts celebrated the rationalism that had emerged through the Enlightenment. However, that rationalism was seen by some to be of a piece with the decadent culture that spawned the Great War. In a reaction to this, there were strong movements against rationalism and Enlightenment aesthetics. The works of the Dadaists sought an anti-aesthetic that would combat the fine culture they associated with the warmongers and weapons manufacturers who had profited from the annihilation of great swathes of a generation of young men. So it was that Dada confronted and challenged the established aesthetic sensibilities of 'high culture'. Whatever one might think of the Dadaists or the coherence of their project, it seems fair to say that the vacuum they created at the heart of modernist aesthetics was filled by the surrealists, who had, and in some cases still have, a positive aesthetic programme with which to pursue their work.

Architecture, again, looks to be left out in the cold. For the other arts, the surrealists celebrated madness, irrationality, primitivism, the unconscious, humour, games, automatic writing and, above all, the dream. These areas of interest to the modernist do not seem compatible with the ambitions of the modern architect, whose work seems to be determined by rational principles. Nevertheless, as we shall see in Chapter 7, the thought that architecture is somehow a mere tool for our use worked out along scientific lines of thought has been challenged by modernists of one stripe or other. We are not only creatures with beliefs; we are also creatures with desires. Architecture, including modern architecture, might be thought to be built in order to help fit the world to the shape of our desires.[4]

Such a conception of architecture allows it into the world of modern art from which it might have been thought to have been excluded. Architecture looks as if it relies upon rational principles in ways in which much of modern art has attempted to resist. However, desires need not conform to rational principles. It was G. E. M. Anscombe, who called our attention to the difference in direction of fit between belief and desire. We change our beliefs in order to make them fit the shape of the world; but we change the shape of the world to fit our desires. Moreover, our beliefs are interconnected in ways which require consistency. Brought to see inconsistency in two of my beliefs I shall feel the pressure of rationality to reconsider their status. If architecture can be connected with desire, it need no longer seek its principles in rationality. No rational constraint is placed upon desire. This way of attaching ourselves to architecture shows that architecture is intimately connected to our mental lives.

We shall look at the relationship between our lives and the environment within which they unfold in further chapters. It is important to know that modernism is not singularly conceived as rationalism; or for that matter, that rationalism should be conceived only as functionalism. Nevertheless, functionalism is persistent as a theory of what it is to be a work of architecture. In the next chapter we consider its merits.

As a visual art, painting was argued to be an example of an art whose works require that we perceive them, and it is in our perception of them that we are able to take an aesthetic interest in them. They are, that is, essentially visual. Such meaning as a painting has, is to be apprehended by looking at it.

Does the parallel case with architecture commit us to functionalism? That is, if we understand architecture as a *visual art*, are we committed to its purpose, its function, being revealed to us in its visual appearance?

In this chapter we have looked at modernism as a development of thought that emerged during the Enlightenment. We have looked particularly at philosophical modernism and yet we have had little to say about modernism in architecture. That is in part because we shall move on to discuss functionalism in the next chapter, where that is to be conceived as one major driving force behind modernist architecture. However, it might be helpful to bring the story of modernism in philosophy to bear upon matters more immediately architectural.

In so doing I want to set the stage for the discussion of function within modernism.

Once asked by a magazine editor to name his favourite chair, le Corbusier cited the seat of a cockpit, and described the first time he ever saw an aeroplane, in the spring of 1909, in the sky above Paris – it was the aviator the Comte de Lambert taking a turn around the Eiffel Tower – as the most significant moment of his life. He observed that the requirements of flight of necessity rid aeroplanes of all superfluous decoration and so unwittingly transformed them into successful pieces of architecture. To place a Classical statue atop a house was as absurd as to add one to a plane, he noted, but at least by crashing in response to this addition, the plane had the advantage of rendering its absurdity starkly manifest.[5]

CHAPTER 3

FUNCTIONALISM

I

In characterizing our standard response to painting as a dependent aesthetic response, we saw that it is not just that the painting is a beautiful object *and* that it depicts some object, person or scene. Rather, we had to say that it is a beautiful painting *in that* it depicts that object, person or scene. Its beauty is grounded in the internal relation between the painting as object; and its depicted content. The conception of the object as a representational painting constrains our judgement of beauty, limiting it to a judgement of dependent beauty. We have in mind the nature of painting and the perfection that might be expected of it as a work of art representing this particular object, person or scene. As a visual art, its appearance is essential to its aesthetic character. What, then of architecture?

A work of architecture, let us say a building, is a beautiful building in that its being designed to serve our purposes constrains our response to it as a beautiful object. In making the analogous case with painting, we might go on to say that it is not that the building is a beautiful object *and* it serves to fulfil some purpose or other. Rather, we want to make the claim that it is a beautiful building *in that* the purpose it serves (or *that* it serves a purpose) internally relates the look of the building to that purpose. That way of putting the matter prevents us from thinking that architecture is a mere formal arrangement of planes, volumes, lines and apertures – a pure beauty that we might, by chance, go on to inhabit. Following Kant, we can say that sculpture is not merely the pursuit of making beautiful arrangements of planes, volumes, lines and spaces. Rather, it is *as sculpture* that we must think of these formal properties as providing a basis upon which to make judgements of beauty. For Kant, sculpture too was a representational art. And so the formal elements of sculpture are to be seen in their contribution to the representational whole. If our conception of sculpture no longer accords with this, we need to circumscribe in what way we are to see the essential nature of sculpture. How does a work's being a sculpture constrain our appreciation of it?

However abstract architecture might be thought to be, it is not to be thought of as abstract sculpture. The parallel with painting brings us to see that buildings are not merely beautiful abstract sculptures that we inhabit. But rather they are beautiful buildings in that our thoughts upon their habitation are directed upon, and in some part constitute, the appearance of the building as works of architecture.

The mention of abstract sculpture would have been entirely foreign to Kant. However, as was mentioned above, Kant thought of 'music without a theme' as a purely formal beauty. If that thought could be stretched to include abstract sculpture, we might permit that there could be works of three-dimensional abstract art that have purely formal aesthetic characteristics. If this were to be so, we could imagine that a sculpture of this order would be considered as having a visual form which alone constitutes the sculpture's appearance. However, even if this were permissible, it would leave architecture as a visual art constrained by the thought that its instances are required to fulfil our purposes. The permeation of our thoughts about architecture by such conceptual constraints gives us grounds for regarding architecture as a fixed or adherent beauty. That the aesthetic character of architecture is so constrained is confirmed by reconsidering the book. The novel has its aesthetic character determined not by the book which houses it; but rather by the development of the story, the plot, the character and the moral insight it affords, among other things. The beauty of the book as a novel is, as we have seen, relatively independent of its housing. This could not be the case with architecture. The look of the object, the building under consideration, is not independent of the aesthetic character of the work of architecture. The look of the building is just what affords the building its aesthetic character. The *visuality* of the building is the location of its aesthetic interest. (We shall consider below various suggestions as to how buildings are to be thought of in terms of language.)

In distinguishing architecture from sculpture, it is clear that works of architecture are constrained by an understanding of them as functional objects, designed for our use. That is, buildings are pressed into our service and it is, at least in part, in respect of their fitness for purpose that we come to appreciate them. As Kant puts it:

> The beauty of a ... building (such as a church, palace, armoury, or summer house) does presuppose the concept of the purpose that

determines what the thing is [meant] to be, and hence a concept of its perfection, and so it is merely adherent beauty.[1]

And again:

> In architecture the main concern is what use is to be made of the artistic object, and this use is a condition to which the aesthetic ideas are confined.[2]

It is, as we have seen, the confinement of aesthetic ideas to the condition of use that requires attention in our appreciation of architecture; and so architecture cannot be understood in the same way as sculpture.

Functionalism is a doctrine, or group of doctrines, that addresses this individuating feature of architecture. Functionalism takes seriously the second of the questions asked at the outset of our study. It provides an account of what is peculiar to architecture in the way in which it engenders our understanding. But it has two ideals of what that understanding is. The first of these regards functionalism as the ground for our aesthetic understanding, while the second simply rejects *aesthetic* understanding in favour of social science. Architectural theorists often vacillate between the two standpoints, and it is difficult to see clearly where the lines are drawn. Moreover, the claims of the functionalists are often, if not always, inconsistent. Nevertheless, functionalism in one form or another has exerted an enormous influence over architectural practice, its history and its theory.

Functionalism, in both its strands, can be seen to have developed from the structural rationalism to be found in the writings of Viollet-le-Duc, the nineteenth-century architect and writer:

> There are in architecture ... two indispensable ways in which truth must be adhered to. We must be true in respect of the programme, and true in respect of the constructive processes. To be true in respect of the programme is to fulfil exactly, scrupulously, the conditions imposed by the requirements of the case. To be true in respect of the constructive processes is to employ the materials according to their qualities and properties.[3]

He goes on to recommend that 'artistic' considerations of symmetry and apparent form are only secondary in the presence of these two dominant principles. What emerged from Viollet-le-Duc's *Discourses* was a commitment to architecture which 'expressed' the programme and the structure of the building. Nevertheless, such expression is to be *seen* in the building under review, and it is a mark of a work's success that we can come to regard it as adhering to these principles. But such a regard is only really coherent if the 'truth' of the building shows up in our experience. Viollet-le-Duc's conception of architecture was, therefore, an aesthetic conception, since it makes claims about how a building can be properly conceived and appreciated in accordance with recommendations of appropriateness.

One strand of modernism arising from this background regards the function of a building as determining its form, so that the form of the building is aesthetically conceived as being appropriate to the utility for which the building was designed. According to this view, the beauty of a building is to be assessed in terms of its form in relation to its function. That is, we must consider the utility of a building when considering the aptness of its form. So a building can have this further value added to its utility, and this further value is, in some specifiable way, to be determined by the building's utility. This way of putting the matter immediately demonstrates its appeal. For we can now, at a stroke, answer both questions with which we began this book. Architecture is the *art* of building. Further, it peculiarly engages our aesthetic understanding by its functional aspect prescribing its form. And this functional prescription just is what provides architecture with its status as an art. Our responses to works of architecture constrain us to *see* how the built form is appropriate to the purpose of the building. Rather than reducing 'artistic' concerns to secondary status, the expression of function becomes the peculiar aesthetic consideration intrinsic to works of architecture.

However, the notion of function, as the basis upon which to build functionalism is far from clear. Adrian Forty, in his scholarly work tracing the ways in which language has been applied to architecture[4] provides us with six different ways in which the term was introduced into the architectural vocabulary and which sustain six different ways of inflecting the term. The six different ways are headed, '1. As a mathematical metaphor'; '2. As a biological metaphor, descriptive of the purposes of the parts of the construction relative to each other and to the whole'; '3. As a biological metaphor within the "organic" theory of form'; '4. "Function" meaning "Use"'; '5. "Functional" as the translation of the German words "*sachlich*", "*zweckmässig*", "*funktionell*"'; and '6. "Function" in the English-speaking world 1930–60.' It is with 2, 3, and 4 that we might best take a philosophical perspective upon function in our conception of architecture as an art.

AESTHETICS AND ARCHITECTURE

Roger Scruton, in his sustained rejection of modernism complains that the dictum, 'form follows function'[5] can be given no coherent meaning.

> What ... is meant by the term 'function'? Are we referring to the function of the building, or to the function of its parts? If only to the latter, does it suffice that a building should simply display all its functional details, like the tubes and wires which deck out the Centre Pompidou? If that is our ideal of aesthetic excellence, then clearly it would be better to discard aesthetics altogether. But it is only in a very superficial sense that such a building expresses or reveals its function, the function of the building being something quite different from the function of its parts. And the function of the whole building – in this case of the Centre Pompidou – is something indeterminate. In so far as the Centre is in competition with no. 4 Carlton House Terrace (which houses London's moral equivalent, but which was in fact designed as a private house), who can say which building best reveals the given use? And are we to think the Round House Theatre, which presumably goes on 'revealing' or 'following' its past function as a railway shed, must for that reason be compromised in its present employment? Such examples show that the idea of 'the function' of a building is far from clear, nor is it clear how any particular 'function' is to be translated into architectural 'form'. All we can say – failing some more adequate aesthetic theory – is that buildings have uses, and should not be understood as though they did not.[6]

In this extended passage, Scruton draws our attention to a number of problems within what we must now loosely call functionalism. 'Discarding aesthetics altogether' is a gloomy thought that we shall come onto shortly. However, it is with the notion of function in relation of part to whole that we can see the biological analogue. The notion of both form and function comes to us from the ancients. In particular Aristotle who, in his rejection of Platonic idealism, sought to refute Plato's theory of forms. We need not rehearse Aristotle's complaints here. However, a rudimentary outline of Aristotle's conception of form will help us in getting clear about the attraction of functionalism to architects. Aristotle conceived of the form of an object to be that which, conceived apart from its material substratum, provided each thing with its essential identity.

FUNCTIONALISM

What [Aristotle] took over [from Plato] and retained was:

(i) the teleological point of view;
(ii) the conviction that reality lies in form.

He could not give up his sense of the supreme importance of form, with which ... it was natural for the Greeks to include function. To know the matter *out of which* a thing had come to be was only a secondary consideration, since the original matter was something shared by it with other things which had developed differently, whereas to understand it meant to lay bare the characteristics which distinguished it from other things. The definition then must describe the form *into which* it had grown. In that, according to Plato and Aristotle, lay its essence. This question of looking for the essence of things in the 'out of which' or the 'into which' introduces us to a fundamental cleavage of outlook which exists in the present world as in the ancient, among laymen as well as philosophers. Knowing as we do that man has evolved from lower types of life, it is natural for some to say that he is 'after all nothing but' an ape, or even a piece of protoplasm, which has happened to take a certain direction. To others his essence lies in the qualities which now distinguish him from the lower forms of life to which his ancestors belonged. They see it not in what he has left behind, but in his capabilities, both present and future. What he can now do is the important thing – his function, dependent on his form.[7]

There is no doubt that the consideration Aristotle gives to form embraces all material things. In his treatment of biological entities, he is concerned to show that, no matter of what it is that we are constituted, it is in terms of our natures as human beings that we understand our potentialities. That is to say that I am to understand a human being as being constituted by parts which are contributive to the whole. A severed hand is not a hand, in Aristotelian terms. For a hand is only to be understood in terms of a whole human being; and its functional capacity as a hand is determined by the form of the whole human being; perhaps we might go further and say: it is determined by the place that it takes up in a whole human life. The passage quoted from Guthrie could almost, word for word, be a piece of architectural functionalist polemic. It is here that we see that both biological analogies, to which Forty refers, come into focus. In particular, the teleological emphasis provided by those who regard an essence as connected with present and future potentialities, regardless of an ancestry, has something of the modernist's optimism about it. But how does it apply to works of architecture, which are not natural objects and do not have natural essences? It is here that we can see the full force of Scruton's argument. Since there are no architectural essences, of the sort that we might expect to find among natural kinds, there can be no pre-determined form that gives rise to a clear idea of function.

II

A second strand of functionalism deriving from structural rationalism is really a dismissal of aesthetic considerations altogether. (We return to Scruton's gloomy thought.) According to the conception of function as socially determined, we need pay no attention to how the building is seen. Hence the building is a product of its function if it best facilitates the activity for which it is designed. Here we pull into focus Forty's conception of function as use. (For instance, I am unconcerned with the 'look' of my car brakes. My interest is in their capacity to bring my car to a stop when my foot is pressed against the pedal.) The concept of function here is akin to that used in engineering. As such it is not an aesthetic theory at all, but rather regards aesthetics as a separate matter, an accidental bonus at best, entirely irrelevant or even 'false consciousness' at worst. It would be false consciousness because it would direct our attention away from true understanding. Our understanding, on this view, would not be engaged with the appearance of the object, but with the connections and subsequent operations of the various levers and pulleys that constitute the system as a whole.

We rehearsed above, the thought that modernism might take engineering as its model. The accidental bonus would accrue just if engineering were to be of such accord with nature that our works of architecture could be seen as aesthetic independently of the architect's work. What is crucial here, as rehearsed above, is that this way of viewing the matter rejects the idea that architecture is a *visual* art. The engineer is, *ex hypothesi*, unconcerned with the look of the object he designs to fulfil some function.

The second refusal to consider aesthetic judgement in architecture arises from a hard-line political point of view. False consciousness is the phenomenon whereby we systematically mask out of our consciousness truths we would rather not believe. Thus, Marxist thinkers regard our naturalizing history a case of hiding from ourselves the real nature of the socio-economic structure that determines our social and cultural life. Freudians too would have it that our dark sexual motives are hidden beneath more palatable niceties. The existentialists, as we shall see, view the bourgeoisie as engaged in false consciousness, in their refusal to face the repulsive character of the empty world.

The case of false consciousness arises from the political, psychological or moral rejection of high culture mentioned in the last chapter. Unlike the view that engineering is not a visual art, this view claims that the exercise of aesthetic taste is itself of a piece with some ideological trend. The purpose of the pursuit of taste, according to this line of thought, is to mask out of consciousness the true nature of our purposes. Taste, in other words, is really the exercise of power and is recruited to the task of establishing and maintaining the current structure of the political and economic hierarchy.[8] Both views, then, are sceptical towards the idea of an aesthetics of architecture. Each sees what purports to be the aesthetics of a visual art as ungrounded. The argument proceeds by regarding architecture as a branch of engineering. As such, it has had an enormous influence upon architects and architectural theorists. Unlike the view that sees function as a biological metaphor, this view concentrates on a building's use.

That this is an ideal to which modern architects have been inclined can be gleaned from *La Sarraz Declaration* 1928 of CIAM (*Congrès International d'Architecture Moderne*) (CIAM 1979). The declaration emphasized the notion of building rather than that of architecture. It sought to place architecture, not in the context of the broader arts, but in the context of economics, politics and social science. It aimed to replace the work of the craftsman with industrial processes, and sought 'the universal adoption of rationalized production methods'[9] in its efforts to increase housing and supersede the methods of a craft era.

Regarded by many as the home of modernist functionalism, the Bauhaus formed a department of architecture in 1927 under the leadership of the Swiss architect Hannes Meyer. One year later, upon the resignation of Walter Gropius as Director, Meyer succeeded him.

> Meyer organized the Bauhaus into four major departments: architecture (now called 'building' for polemical reasons), advertising, wood and metal production, and textiles. Supplementary scientific courses, such as industrial organization and psychology, were introduced into all departments, while the building section shifted its

emphasis to the economic optimization of plan arrangements and to methods for the precise calculation of light, sunlight, heat loss/gain, and acoustics.[10]

In both the ideological parlance and tone of the declaration, together with the shift in focus of Meyer's Bauhaus, it is clear that aesthetic considerations do not intrude upon the central task of the architect as conceived by this austere strand of functionalism. Architecture, in achieving the status of art, had sought to rise above the humdrum realm of mere building. In a rather ironic, politically driven inversion, however, it is building that comes to occupy the ideological high ground; coming down upon architectural pretension like a ton of bricks.

However, even if such a view were sustainable, it would not fall within the aesthetics of architecture, except as a challenge to provide a positive account that would persuade the spectator that architecture is worth looking at, and that architects can thereby provide works which are valuable in and of themselves. Rather than solving the problem with which we started, austere functionalism refuses to acknowledge there is a problem. It descends from the ethereal air of architecture to the solid ground of mere building. In so doing it thereby provides a criterion by which we measure the successful work: efficiency.

Nevertheless, it is worth noting that at least a sizeable amount of the buildings, furniture and fittings designed by austere functionalists *are worth looking at*. That is, whatever the claims of the designers and their supportive theorists, the look of the works is aesthetically estimable and it seems incredible that this is mere caprice. Austere functionalism, we might think therefore, is a prime example of a critically engaged theory which immunizes its works from *aesthetic* criticism (by removing them from its orbit) and thereby promotes and protects its adherents in their artistic practice. (Much of what has been said in this section is true of all the modern arts, together with the various polemical arguments developed to sustain them; a great deal of which, when *looked at*, turn out to be aesthetically valuable, despite the protestations of the artists and theoreticians who would know better.)

However, in a novel interpretation of architectural history, one commentator sees modernism as derived from the certainties with which engineers made beautiful structures unhindered by worries of style or decoration.[11] De Botton sees the development of modernism in architecture as a natural event brought about by the problem of style – whether to build in the classical or the gothic – at the same time as the industrial revolution made feats of engineering possible, with bridges, railways and other monumental structures being made without recourse to the self-conscious debates concerning style.

According to such a view, aesthetics arises not out of design but out of a strictness in formulating solutions to problems. (This is the engineering view rehearsed above.) This, however, would render the aesthetics of architecture of a piece with the aesthetics of nature. Works of architecture would not count as works of art; but instead they would be regarded as scientific solutions to the problems brought into focus by our need to span rivers, or to hold great quantities of water, or to provide waterway routes between manufacturing cities. They are solutions, that is, to problems that are not intrinsically aesthetic. Hence they should be assessed as natural phenomena, their beauty being independent of their authors' intentions to solve problems. There are, of course, many things that we consider in this way. We consider many man-made items as aesthetic, even though they were not meant to be looked at from an aesthetic point of view. The accidental '*décollage*' that results when old posters are peeled from their billboards partially revealing layers of previous scraps can be astonishingly beautiful. The same is true of peeling wallpaper and chipped paint, as they are to be found in derelict buildings. These are not natural phenomena. They are the result of someone's *doing something*. But the something that is done, is carried out without thought of the resultant beauty that we find in our looking at them from this perspective. Nevertheless, as we have argued above, architecture is best considered a visual art, an art whose instances are brought into being in such a way that both architect and spectator have a sense of them as intended *to be seen*.

Functionalism, under both its aspects we might feel, is inadequate as an account of our aesthetic responses to architecture. For the notion of function, in the context of architecture, remains irredeemably vague. Consider, for instance, the urban design of the square. Take the Plaza Major in Madrid. What is its function? On Tuesdays it is a market, on Saints' days it is a fairground, on Sundays townspeople gather to parade in their finery. In the evenings families meet up for drinks, and on Saturday mornings it becomes a centre for the exchange of rare stamps. When built, it was the palace of the king and was overlooked by courtiers' balconies. It was, at one time, the *plaza de Torres*. During the Inquisition it was used for show trials and ritual executions. It now houses offices and a range of cheap to expensive hotel accommodation, bars and restaurants. That is, the life of its design – the range of activities made available by it – has outstripped any restrictive conception of 'the function' for which it was designed. It seems merely stipulative to deem any of its varied historical uses illegitimate. Moreover, since the business of aesthetics is born of a conception of ourselves as free, we might think it is of the essence of our conception of architectural utility that it should remain irredeemably vague, so that any morally permissible human purpose might be pursued within the designed environment. It remains true that while the fact that a building has utility enters into our conception of the nature of architecture, we cannot be required to specify in detail what particular use a building must have.

There are many uses to which we put bedrooms. Why should we feel constrained to stipulate *the* use? We sleep in them, as well as other places. We make love in them. We give birth in them. We lie up sick in them; and we die in them. We stare at the ceiling in them, while trying to work out the next move in a vexed chapter we are writing. We take refuge in them when we are unable to surmount our regrets; or we drink champagne in bed on the mornings of our birthdays and on other festive occasions. What must we say about the use to which we put our bedrooms? Our failure to be able to answer this question points up the failure of functionalism, in the two forms we have considered, to provide an adequate account of the aesthetics of architecture.

CHAPTER 4

RESIDUAL PROBLEMS: THEORY AND PRACTICE

I

Thus far into our study we have looked at a number of candidates put forward to explain the essential character of architecture. Each holds its own attraction and it is easy to understand how architects – and the theorists who provide them with support – might be persuaded by them. However, none of the views so far has been adequate to the task. Each view, that is, contains and retains residual problems. There is one philosophical problem, however, the consideration of which might cast light upon the theories when grouped together. The problem is this: How is the theory put forward related to the work of architecture that is supported by it? What is the relation between theory and practice?

It is often difficult to tell in which direction influence exerts itself when considering the practices of art and the various theories that form around those practices. At the outset of this book it was claimed that philosophical treatment of the arts in general should ask and seek answers to questions arising from artistic practice at its most abstract. And yet, even at the outset, it was conceded that questions arise naturally from the practice of art and that answers to questions regarding art have consequences for our conception of the art in question; and implications for the practice of that art. There is, we might feel, a two-way traffic connecting practice and theory. Symbiosis suggests itself as a biological metaphor.

Now there seems to be no way of telling, in advance, how much practice should conform to theory, on the one hand; and how much theory should conform to practice, on the other. If the level of abstraction of philosophical aesthetics is to touch upon these matters; and if it is to have some say in how these matters might be resolved, it should call upon resources specifically philosophical. In aiming at consistency and intelligibility; and, perhaps more importantly, in aiming at persuading both theoreticians and practitioners, it must attempt to spell out the consequences of adopting particular theories and particular practices. This is by no means an easy task. In this chapter, we shall consider the disadvantages of holding on to classicism, modernism and functionalism, respectively. In drawing our conclusions, we shall then be in a better position to see how it is that the relation of theory and practice is to be conceived. In the next chapter, we will then be equipped to look at one of the most influential theories that has held sway, to a greater or lesser extent, over all the arts in the second half of the twentieth century and into the present.

We might characterize, if not caricature, two extreme positions, tending toward opposite ends of the spectrum. The one is rehearsed in the presence of some new presentation of avant-garde art, the other, as a rebuttal of the first. 'That isn't art', says a member of an outraged public confronted with the latest offering by some Young Turk. 'It's art if I say it is', replies the Young Turk. On the one hand, the intuition is that this piece of 'art' has gone too far beyond what is, ordinarily speaking, intelligible for it to be included in the realm of art, however that is loosely characterized. In order for the outrage to make sense, the outraged must subscribe to some, even if vague, theory of what constitutes a work of art. On the other, the artist rejects the judgement of others, since his practice abides independently of any theoretical framework, whatever its characterization. Each extreme, it might seem, is a direct expression of a philosophical point of view. The reconciliation of these seemingly intractable positions is the business of this chapter.

II

The case against classicism, which purported to be the one true form of architecture rested on two claims. The first was that architecture is not – at least not a fully fledged – representational art. Some classicists have claimed that our understanding of its works is in our grasp of their mimetic features. That position was rejected in virtue of the fact that representation is an intentional activity. And yet it is plausible to think that some works of classicism exhibit the virtues of that form of architecture while being designed independently of any adherence to the theory that ascribes mimesis to classicist architecture. If that is the case then it is plausible to think that some architect might design a classical building that is elegant, historically pertinent, inventive, dignified and restrained, while having no notion of the representation of the primitive form of building that is supposed to underwrite the practice from a theoretical perspective. That is to say that the work can be a good example of classical architecture without the architect subscribing to the theory that classical architecture is mimetic.

What now can the theorist say in rejoinder? He can always say that this is not a piece of classicism; but that seems a rather desperate measure under the circumstances. He could argue against the view that representation is intentional; maintaining that the work under consideration *is* mimetic, whether or not the architect subscribes to the view or not. However, this seems a dangerous move. It would mean that the theoretician knows better than the practitioner what the practitioner is doing. That is not an illogical move. However, if the practitioner is made aware of the theory and remains unconvinced that his work is mimetic, the theoretician is in a position of holding onto the theory against considerable odds. His theory, that is, becomes stipulative rather than descriptive. Its status as a theory changes.

Notwithstanding the argument against the mimetic treatment of classicism, there is a more serious objection with which it has to contend. The classicist claims that classicism is the only way in which to build. If that is so, how is he able to deal with works of architecture that do not conform to the strictures of classicism? Both within and beyond the western tradition, there is a history of traditions that place building at the centre of a culture as a visual art. The classicist seems to be forced to deem these other buildings non-architectural. But again, this seems to be merely stipulative. The fact that we want to understand architecture at its broadest should lead us to consider the designed world of contemporary peoples and the traditions from which they have emerged. While it may well be that classicism recommends itself as the most beautiful or sensitive or dignified way to build, that is a matter of taste and it is not for the philosopher to legislate over these matters.[1]

For the philosopher to say of a supposed work of architecture that it is not architecture requires of him an explanation as to why we might be persuaded so. In rejecting the hastily built and ill-considered dog-kennel, he might tell us that the object was built without consideration for how it looks. The look of the kennel did not shape or guide the builder's intentions when the kennel was being built. From this we might be persuaded that the look of a building has to be considered by the designer; and that considerations of how the building shall look serve to organize and regulate the fabrication of the building. That is to say that we can be persuaded by such cases, that *why* it is that our intuitions rule against the admission of the kennel to the realm of architecture is that an important feature of our conception of architecture is missing.

At one stage in the history of painting, abstract art was rejected. The reason for its rejection was that it had failed to observe its representational duties. The ensuing argument sought to adjudicate between those who felt that representation was an essential feature of painting; and those who sought to show that representation was only contingently connected to the art. Each view adopts a theoretical position with regard to painting; and each calls upon our intuitions in attempting to establish its thesis.

With regard to classicism, it is surely too constrained a view that it alone is the true form of architecture. That would render great buildings from outwith the western tradition non-architectural. It would also severely restrict what would count as architecture from within the western tradition. If the conservative classicist is correct, then the works of Pugin, Le Corbusier, Rietveld, Mies van der Rohe, Frank Lloyd Wright, J. J. P. Oud and others, are to be rejected. It is not illogical to maintain the conservative classicist view. It remains, however, unpersuasive, to say the least.

III

We looked at modernism as that has grown out of the Enlightenment. Modernism is less governable than classicism, more unruly – being a ragbag of tendencies, some half formed, some not even that. There seems to be little to unite the various trends that comprise modernism in the arts. In the visual fine arts we have Fauvism, Expressionism, Cubism, Purism, Orphism, Futurism, Vorticism, Dada, Surrealism, Suprematism, De Stijl, Constructivism, Op Art, Pop Art, Minimalism and so on. These movements tend to pull against one another and yet all are somehow to be included in modernist art. In architecture there is Structural Rationalism, Futurism, Classical Rationalism, European Architectural Expressionism, Formalism, De Stijl, National Romanticism, The International Style, The New Brutalism, Critical Regionalism and more beside. Nevertheless, what these movements and 'isms' have in common, across the visual arts, is a propensity to rest upon theoretical foundations. Art and architecture of the modern period have become intrinsically theoretical.

RESIDUAL PROBLEMS

It is at this point that we ought to beware of our earlier suggestion that symbiosis is the biological metaphor appropriate to the relationship we are seeking to clarify. For, in biology, symbiosis is a relation held between two (or more) organisms whose mutual benefit is profitably pursued in the relationship. We think of the two species as organic partners whose mutual flourishing is secured in the relationship that each enters into with the other. That is to say that both partners in the relationship are regarded as having a similar status, each relying upon the other whilst at the same time supporting its well-being. However apt this might be as a model for the understanding of the relationship held between theory and practice in the arts, we should remember that theory and practice have separate aims and that these aims furnish each with a different status.

Theory, at least on the face of it, aims at truth. Its pronouncements aim to explain that which is otherwise mysterious or confused; or it provides means by which works of art can be better understood. The practice of visual art, at least as traditionally conceived, is to provide works that engage our sensibilities by means of securing experiences in which we are able to *see* and value aspects of our condition. That may put it rather grandly, but the point is that theory aims at truth, whereas visual art, and the arts more generally, aim at value; and at value embedded in aesthetic experience.

The point of seeking out the truth is to expand our knowledge of the world and to widen the network of beliefs through which we are able to grasp that world. (Of course, in seeking the truth we might also need to reject views we had hitherto taken to be true. We might, that is, be required to constrict our network of beliefs through which we attempt to grasp the world.) The writing of a poem or a sonata, by contrast does not aim to widen or constrict our network of beliefs. It aims at something quite different. The making of art aims at widening the range of valuable objects that we are able to encounter in terms of the experiences they afford. Thus art and theory have different *kinds* of aim.

Here we might remind ourselves of Kant's three critiques. It was in order to explain how reason could engage in the pursuit of different rational aims that Kant developed his philosophy. Theoretical reason is undertaken in order for us to move from beliefs about the world to new beliefs about the world. The conclusion of theoretical reason is belief. Practical reason is undertaken to persuade us to act in ways according to the moral law. The conclusion of practical reason is action. Critical reason persuades us to *see* the world under a certain light. The conclusion of critical reasoning is experience.

The problem that arises for modernist art, emerging from modernist philosophy, then, is that theory and practice aim at different conclusions; and therefore the status of a work of art is dissimilar to that of a piece of theory. The visual arts, in general, and architecture in particular, in so far as they are part of an aesthetic project, aim at making significantly beautiful objects; objects that afford experiences through which we are able to arrive at a sense of value. Theory, on the other hand, aims at making sense of that which constitutes art and architecture; and aims at clarification as to how they should be practised. This is just to repeat that practice aims at beauty, whereas theory aims at truth.

We shall return to this difference in the next two chapters, where we shall call upon resources in the philosophy of mind to cast light upon the important differences between certain mental attributes; and to call into focus such problems as befall those who have no such resources to hand. Suffice it to say for now, that truth and belief on the one hand, and imagination and experience on the other, are to be given quite different treatments. And that a good deal follows from their various treatments that concerns aesthetics and art; and architecture; and their theories.

What then of the intimate relation demanded in modernist movements between theory and practice? We have noted that the various works within their various movements rely upon the theoretical support of the movement in order to position themselves within the intellectual and aesthetic context required by modernism. What then must we think of the artwork whose theoretical support is undermined. Since the theory aimed at truth, it is always possible that it can be shown to be false. Should this happen, however, it does not follow that the work of art produced within the movement, supported by the falsified theory, has its status as a beautiful work of art withdrawn. Examples abound. However, one need look no further than the late theosophist paintings of Piet Mondrian or the work of the pointillists in order to see that the theories have been discarded without loss of value to the works themselves.

This puzzle can be resolved; and in its resolution we can look in either of two opposite directions. We can reject the aesthetic aim of art and architecture, thereby turning our attention to the theory and consigning associated practical work to the drawer marked 'historically interesting'. More persuasively, however, I think it is plausible to turn our attention toward works of art and architecture. After all, we do value and appreciate works of art from previous periods in ways which are characterized aesthetically. Take some examples. We do not attend the concert hall to listen to Beethoven's Ninth because it is of historical interest to us; nor do we visit the Prado Museum in Madrid to look at Goya's '*Black Paintings*' because we are captivated by the madness that seized him late in life. The pleasure that is enjoyed when watching the sunlight glint off the upper levels of William van Alen's Chrysler Building in New York is not confined to an interest in the early part of the last century. In each case our *aesthetic* interest is aroused in appreciating the music, the paintings and the architecture, respectively.

How then are we to characterize our interest in the theoretical aspect in its relationship with the practice of art and architecture? What are we to make of the theory that we no longer find persuasive? It is here that modernism itself, broadly conceived, proves fruitful. We have already considered the familiar notion that modernism concerns itself, within each of the arts, with the features essential to those arts. Modernist arts, that is, take on a theoretical stance toward their own practice. This is true of each of the movements within the visual fine arts and within each of the factions within modern architecture.

In order to understand some movement or other, then, a spectator is expected to engage with the theoretical structure that supports and sustains it. However, if that theoretical position is not aimed at truth, but is rather to be thought of as part of the content of the work under view, then we need not worry about the suppositions of the theory turning out false. Of course, it might well be that, *psychologically*, the theory has to be *believed* by the artist or architect in order for that artist or architect to be able to pursue the work in hand. That is, it might be a psychological requirement of the practice, that the theory is taken to be true by the artist or architect. However, if the spectator regards the theory not as a commitment to truth, but rather as a necessary theoretical perspective the artist or architect has upon their work, he will be able to appreciate the work by including the theoretical perspective within his aesthetic appreciation, independently of any truth claim that the attendant theory might make. That is, in appreciating the work of the austere functionalists, for example, I am to consider the theoretical aspects of their work, not in terms of the truth of functionalism, but in terms of the contribution of the theory to the visual experience the work affords. That is, by entertaining the theoretical aspect, the spectator need not judge it in terms of its veracity. Rather, he should allow the entertainment of the aspect to suffuse the experience he has in front of the work under view. In a word, the theoretical aspect gets accommodated, independently of its truth or falsehood, in the imagination of the spectator.

That this is a contentious view should be immediately apparent. For it implies that theory has no independent status; and has its standing delivered by the art in which in has been internalized. In removing theory from the realm of truth value, we seem to put it at too remote a distance from those branches of thought concerning the abstract nature of art and architecture; that is, the philosophy of art or aesthetics. I think there is some truth in this; and it is a corollary of that truth that we should not expect to find that the philosophy of art has much to say by way of recommending this or that movement within the arts. However, the broad truths it delivers might well engage with the theories of modern art and architecture if the theoretical aspect threatens to become too dominant in the pursuit of practice. We shall return to this notion, in Chapters 5 and 6, when we come to consider possibly the most dominant theoretical positions emerging from the twentieth century – structuralism and post-structuralism.

IV

Functionalism, and in particular the notion that form follows function, was seen to fail because we do not, when pressed, have sufficient grasp of what is a building's function; and since buildings are not natural kinds and cannot be treated as if they are, we have no sense of what it is for a function to prescribe a form. Functionalism, like classicism and formalist modernism, restricts too narrowly what we would be permitted to admit as works of architecture. For surely, no adequate theory of architecture could rule inadmissible the works of the great German baroque architects, or the Spanish or Italians for that matter. The extraordinary solemnity of Nicholas Hawksmoor's St Anne's in Limehouse, together with his other masterpieces dotted around London's East End, would have to be rejected as failing to properly express their function. And so we see that contemporary theories of architecture, while required to promote the work of architects, need not be taken too seriously when considering the larger picture. The grand claims of the classicists; those of the modern formalists; and those of the various stripes of functionalism, should be entertained as ways of perceiving the works that have emerged in the struggle to make architecture. It is not that theory should be taken with a pinch of salt. Rather, we should take the arts generally, and architecture in particular, with the rich seasoning that theory provides.

PART II

THEORY IN ARCHITECTURE

CHAPTER 5

STRUCTURALIST ACCOUNTS

I

In Chapter 2, we looked at the philosophical developments emerging from the Enlightenment. The modern period, as we saw, began to view the world from a scientific point of view. It was upon the seat of reason that humanity rested its hopes, having wearied from kneeling at the throne of the Almighty. Our hopes come to rest upon intellection, not genuflection; upon the history of natural selection, rather than the mystery of the resurrection. Thus the certainties of reason and the methods engaged in their acquisition became the accepted means by which knowledge might be pursued. Science promised the eventual mastery of all knowledge; and thus anything that presented itself as either problem or puzzle would find itself subjected to the scrutiny of the relevant science. The natural sciences comprised physics, chemistry and biology; and any questions demanding answers from beyond their scope would nevertheless require scientific methodology in order to broaden the frontiers of knowledge. So it was that new sciences, the human or social sciences – psychology, sociology, anthropology and linguistics, for instance – appeared as disciplines in their infancy.

It is against this background that we can understand the importance of one of three modern innovative thinkers, born within two years of each other; and each of whose works straddle the cusp of the nineteenth and twentieth centuries. Sigmund Freud was born in 1856, Emile Durkheim and Ferdinand de Saussure in 1857. Each has had a remarkable influence in their own field of social science; each his impact upon the humanities; and each has had an enormous influence on our thinking about the theory of the arts. For present purposes, we shall be concerned with the thought of Ferdinand de Saussure, the Swiss linguist, whose work lies at the very heart of structuralism and its development into the centre and then out toward the further stretches of cultural studies; contemporarily reaching the heart of the relatively new discipline, visual theory.

Published posthumously in Geneva in 1915, Saussure's lectures across 5 years of teaching at the University of Geneva (1906–11) were written up by two of his colleagues, from the lecture notes taken by his students.[1] In *Course in General Linguistics*, Saussure presages the advent of semiology as one of the new social sciences:

> It is . . . possible to conceive of a science *which studies the role of signs as part of social life*. It would form part of social psychology, and hence of general psychology. We shall call it *semiology* (from the Greek *sēmeîon*, 'sign '). It would investigate the nature of signs and the laws governing them. Since it does not exist, one cannot say for certain that it will exist. But it has a right to exist, a place ready for it in advance. Linguistics is only one branch of this general science. The laws which semiology will discover will be laws applicable in linguistics, and linguistics will thus be assigned to a clearly defined place in the field of human knowledge.[2]

In recent modernist and postmodernist orthodoxy much weight is put on the concept of a sign and of signification in art.[3] It is with signification that the orthodoxy claims to give an account of meaning for the arts. Saussure's definition of a sign is vague in terms of its semantic import. This is because he is not concerned with particular usage of language but with its structure. A sign, according to him, is comprised of two parts, the signifier (*signifiant*) and the signified (*signifié*).[4] The signifier is the spoken word composed of phonemes and forming a sound pattern of the word when spoken (i.e. the physical aspect of the unit as perceived). The signified, however, is not the referent of the word, but is the concept to which the word is attached by convention. So, the word 'tree' is a particular sound pattern as it vibrates on the air, and its signified is the *concept* 'tree'. No tree is referred to in this system and so the world drops out of consideration at an early stage. 'The linguistic sign unites, not a thing and a name, but a concept and a sound pattern.'[5]

Taking the language as a whole, each unit has its specific place which is defined in opposition to all other units. Thus, for a unit to have meaning it must be identifiable as *that* unit belonging here rather than there in the language matrix. In order to get clear about this idea we might take an example. Imagine a jig-saw puzzle, each of whose pieces is unique in shape. The formal place that each is assigned in the system, is specified according to its constitutive role in the complex whole. Moreover, the pieces might be considered independently of the 'picture' which they support or comprise when correctly put together. (We could, for instance, put the puzzle

STRUCTURALIST ACCOUNTS

together following two principles. Either we could use the picture as a guide, as puzzle solvers usually do in correctly putting the pieces together; or we could use the shape and structure of the pieces independently of any pictorial composition; or we could use some amalgam of these two principles.) The same pattern of individual shapes could be used to ground more than one picture. The piece might be thought of as being defined by its opposition to the positions of the other pieces in the puzzle. It finds its place (its place is defined for it) by its particular shape. Similarly, the sound pattern 'pan' has one set of oppositions in English but has another in Spanish. It has a specific shape in the 'sound dictionary' so to speak. The English and Spanish 'sound dictionaries' are just the complete set of sound combinations which amount to the oppositions within which this particular sound pattern is located.

For actual languages Saussure posited two dimensions along which the system of meaning depended. The first of these is the *syntagmatic* dimension, along which the strings of phonemes and hence of recognizable words is unfolded in time: roughly, sentences. The second is the *paradigmatic* dimension or, as it is sometimes referred to, the associative. Here the connection is made between the unit of meaning and other units of meaning associated with it by the language user: for instance 'cat' might be paradigmatically related to 'kitten' and to 'feline mammal'.

Here is Saussure on the difference between these two dimensions:

> In a linguistic state, then, everything depends on relations. How do they work?
>
> The relations and differences between linguistic items fall into two quite distinct kinds, each giving rise to a separate order of values. The opposition between these two orders brings out the specific character of each. They correspond to two different forms of mental activity, both indispensable to the workings of language.
>
> Words as used in discourse, strung together one after another, enter into relations based on the linear character of languages. Linearity precludes the possibility of uttering two words simultaneously. They must be arranged consecutively in spoken sequence. Combinations based on sequentiality may be called *syntagmas*. The syntagma invariably comprises two or more consecutive units ... In its place in a syntagma, any unit acquires its value simply in opposition to what precedes, or to what follows, or both.[6]

Saussure locates syntagmatic 'value' in the place that a unit (a word) takes up in the sequence of the sentence. Since I cannot at one and the same time say both 'cat' and 'kitten', only one of these can sit properly in the sequence of signs that forms the sentence, 'The cat wants milk'. But here, the relationship that the word 'cat' has to 'The', 'wants' and 'milk', respectively, is syntagmatic; since it is this sequence of other words that holds the place for 'cat' in the sentence. It is in opposition to these other words that 'cat' finds its place, so to speak.

If this is an adequate account of language, it is easy to see how architecture could be seen to exhibit a structural counterpart of language. Since Saussure is not concerned with language–world relations, the fact that buildings have regular identifiable components makes it easy, at first sight, to speak of the language of architecture; and the vocabulary of architecture. Windows, doors, roofs and staircases seem to exhibit the same sort of relational properties as do the purported syntagms in Saussure's system.

On the other hand:

> Outside the context of discourse, words having something in common are associated together in the memory. In this way they form groups, the members of which may be related in various ways.[7]

So, for instance, the relation between the two words 'cat' and 'kitten' is held to be one of association, secured by their commonality or connection in memory.

> This kind of connexion between words is of a quite different order. It is a connexion in the brain [sic!]. Such connexions are part of that accumulated store which is the form the language takes in an individual's brain. We shall call these *associative relations*.
>
> Syntagmatic relations hold in *praesentia*. They hold between two or more terms co-present in a sequence. Associative relations, on the contrary, hold in *absentia*. They hold between terms constituting a mnemonic group.[8]

It is difficult to get a clear view of what is being claimed here. However, perhaps we might be tempted to think of the relation between the building, at which we look, and other buildings from the history of architecture. That is to say that the relation between the building in front of us to architectural history brings the 'absent' to

STRUCTURALIST ACCOUNTS

bear upon that which is 'present'; and so here we have a counterpart to the paradigmatic or associative relation.

Given Saussure's conception of the individual sign as being relatively independent of the world and his view that the signifier and signified are related arbitrarily, it follows that the dimension of syntagmatic relations offers the most secure basis for structural analysis. The associative relations, by contrast, have their seat 'in the brain'. For each there will be any number of associations that can be generated from any one sign. However, it is impossible to legislate what these associative relations will be for any particular language speaker, when in the process of associating any one sign with its relations along this axis of 'meaning'. Saussure offers no argument for the systematic analysis of the associative but claims that the mind 'contrives to introduce a principle of order' which will thereby limit the arbitrariness of the associative bundle.

Here is a synopsis of Saussure's view on the two dimensions provided by Stuart Sim:

> To summarise the main points of Saussure's argument: language is a self-contained system consisting of signs. Signs consist of a signifier and a signified. The sign is arbitrary, signifier and signified having no necessary connection with each other; although once the system is in operation the human disposition towards patterning will have the effect of imposing a sense of order and coherence on signs. Within any system, meaning is conventional ... Relations are either syntagmatic ... or paradigmatic (associative) ... Linguistics is the study of language-systems and it provides a methodological model for the study of all other systems. It is to be subsumed in its turn under the more general science of semiotics, the study of signs and how they operate within systems.[9]

II

With this sketch of the fundamental thought from which structuralism emerged before us, we can move on to ask why such a theory is attractive to artists, architects and their critics. Before so doing, however, we must first note an ambiguity within structuralism, equivocation over which, I believe, provides the basis for a particular version of aesthetic modernism.

Sim's emphasis is on the *scientific* nature of structuralism. Two of the examples he uses to illustrate structuralism in practice, however, become confused on this point. We are to consider the work of Vladimir Propp with regard to Russian folktales and that of Lévi-Strauss and his treatment of South American Indian myths. Propp introduces the notion of 'transformation' in which we notice certain constants in the folktales under review: that there is a landscape, that there is a setting, that there are characters and so forth. However, in the individual folktale these constants undergo a transformation so that in *this* tale the character wears *this* form of dress, the setting is in *this* house within a particular landscape and so on. In short, we notice a unifying structure *in* the tales and see that this structure is transformed in each particular tale by its local character.

In the work of Lévi-Strauss we are to see the unity *beneath* the appearances in the divergent Indian myths. At first sight these two enterprises may look similar in form. Of his own work in structural anthropology, Lévi-Strauss claims that:

> [The only justification] lies in the unique and most economical coding system to which it can reduce messages of a most disheartening complexity, *and which previously appeared to defeat all attempts to decipher them*. Either structural analysis succeeds in exhausting all concrete modalities of its subject, or we lose the right to apply it to one of the modalities. (my emphasis)[10]

Here Lévi-Strauss regards his work as finding the structural unity beneath the appearance. In the true spirit of scientific enquiry he is concerned to grasp the explanatory unity notwithstanding the diversity of appearance. It is not clear in Propp's case that this is the general aim. For instance, it is utterly obvious that the folktales contain characters, landscapes and settings. The unifying structure here is not hidden beneath the surface appearance but is rather part of the description of that appearance.

Propp's work provides the basis of one strand of formalist criticism in literature, but while form and content might be described independently of one another, the form *together with* the content are part of the description of the work as it appears to us. Formalist criticism is not scientific in the way in which Lévi-Strauss' anthropology seeks to be understood. What is important in Propp's work is the difference between two folktales. Each tale is then understood and appreciated as a unique work of art (albeit as a variation on some common theme). What is important about Lévi-Strauss' work is the similarity between two (seemingly) disparate Indian myths. The unity beneath the apparent surface of the two myths is discovered by the 'scientist' and this unity then provides an explanation in general of some feature common to both. In Propp's case we move from the *surface unity* to notice the individuating features of each folktale. In Lévi-Strauss the direction moves from the particular surface features of the myth to the deep unity which was hitherto hidden.

Why should equivocation over these two kinds of structural unity attract art and architectural theorists? On the one hand it provides criticism and theory of art and architecture with scientific credentials and with what would seem to be a solid methodology for research into art and architecture and their histories. It would make art and architecture intellectually serious on a footing with science. On the other hand it appears to have an explanatory dimension when taken to be descriptive of the appearance of works of art and architecture. We notice the differences and seem to have a grasp of the individuality of a work of art while at the same time seeing it as part of a more general scheme. So, we look at a Picasso cubist painting noticing the features which make it a cubist painting *in general*, while at the same time we are able to see how this particular painting has transformed the still life. We look at a work within the de Stijl movement and see how Gerhardt Rietveld has transformed that version of modernism into his particular building.

Consider, for example, the Volkswagen Beetle. If we were to look at the range of models of this car since it was first produced we would notice that there is an overall similarity in the shape of the car. While at the same time we would pay attention to the particular details 'transformed' in each particular version of the model. However, there is nothing to discover beneath the surface appearance of the collection of Beetles. We simply see the unity which makes the Beetle recognizable in each of the models. Perhaps, then, we might think that structuralist linguistics, with its conception of signification, does not furnish us with a science of meaning but with a picture of how the distinctions between works of art and architecture might be mapped along Propp's formalist lines. So, following Propp's methodology, we might come to see stylistic unity together with its 'rules' of inclusion as being usefully explained by the surface structure demonstrated by the theorist. It remains, however, a moot point as to whether the structuralist working along these lines lends anything additional of value to the art historian concerned with grouping works according to style. That is, grouping works of art and architecture stylistically seems to be no more or less than Propp's project as I have characterized it. As such, there is nothing added to the work of the stylistic historian by the framework provided by structuralism. This is no more than, and no less than, the interpretative history of art.

The ideas of appearance and hidden depth need more attention. We shall return to these matters in Part III. For now, however, we can say roughly: that which is apparent includes not only that which we actually see at any one time. But it also includes that which we can be brought to see. The importance lies in the *phenomenological* character of the agreement we are able to come to when we consider the properties under the light of criticism. 'Now I see it' relies upon the spectator having an experience of the work. The spectator can come to have experiences on the basis of persuasion. However, the last criterion of the spectator's agreement is in his having an experience with a certain content.

Here we might remember the position set out in the last chapter, where we considered the idea that theory might not aim at truth, but might itself be included in the content of the experience of the work of architecture. Theory, on this view, does not so much state: 'This artwork means such and such'. Rather, it suggests: 'Why don't you look at the building under this directive?' The first of these theoretical pronouncements makes a truth claim. The second does not. If we take the attempts to give structuralist analysis as interpretative in the spirit of art history as traditionally conceived, we might then see why they are so persuasive. Barthes writes persuasively, if not conclusively, on a number of visual artefacts in his book *Mythologies*, which includes an essay on the Eiffel Tower. In that essay much of what he has to say is illuminating, suggestive, intriguing, entertaining and permits the reader to ride along with the currents and eddies that provide the essay with its broad sweep. However, this is not enough for the semiologist, who insists that the project is scientific in its nature; and thereby truth seeking in its status. Here is Barthes in a lecture entitled 'Semiology and the Urban' delivered in 1967 to the *Institut Français*:

> The city is a discourse and this discourse is truly a language: the city speaks to its inhabitants, we speak our city, the city where we are, simply by living in it, by wandering through it, by looking at it. Still the problem is to bring an expression like 'the language of the city' out of the purely metaphorical stage. It is very easy metaphorically to speak of the language of the city as we speak of the language of the cinema or the language of flowers. The real scientific leap will be realized when we speak of a language of the city without metaphor.[11]

STRUCTURALIST ACCOUNTS

Barthes was a luminary of the structuralist and semiological tendency. Like other intellectuals writing within and on the nature of their discipline, architecture is to be considered a field of enquiry or a field of operation within which to apply the methods of the new science. What might we find within the practice of architecture that reveals the influence of this thought upon the built environment?

Rejecting the old guard constitutive of the previous CIAM, a number of younger architects wrote in response to the CIAM VIII report. Among their number was the Dutch architect, Aldo van Eyck. The young architects, later given responsibility for CIAM X (which was to disband CIAM and inaugurate Team X) wrote:

> Man may readily identify himself with his own hearth, but not easily with the town within which it is placed. 'Belonging' is a basic emotional need – its associations are of the simplest order. From 'belonging' – identity – comes the enriching sense of neighbourliness. The short narrow street of the slum succeeds where spacious redevelopment frequently fails.[12]

Van Eyck had been strongly influenced by Lévi-Strauss' structuralist anthropology, and had undertaken his own field-trips to study the indigenous shelters of the Dogon people of north-west Africa. In dismissing the rationalism of the functionalist city, van Eyck sought to posit a structure that would demonstrate the congruence of the social fabric and its architectural counterpart. Van Eyck's students took up the cause and designed architecture that would exemplify structures of social organization in its built form. The best examples of this work, *as work developed from a theoretical position*, are perhaps van Eyck's Children's Orphanage, in Amsterdam, 1960, and his student Hermann Hertzberger's Central Beheer, in Apeldoorn, 1967–70.

Whether or not these buildings stand up to architectural criticism, relies less upon the truth of structuralism and more upon the very clear intuitions that van Eyck vented when he put his name to the reply to CIAM VIII. How much the clarity of that piece of writing shows up in the architecture is another matter. We return now to the more theoretical basis upon which this structuralist architecture was grounded.

AESTHETICS AND ARCHITECTURE

III

Saussure had insisted, and correctly so, that our ability to discern phonemic structures requires that we recognize units of meaning such that they are reiterable. This is a recognitional capacity and so it is based in perception. Saussure did not think it necessary to distinguish between understanding language, where that consists in mastery of concepts and grasping content on the one hand; and investing perception with significance on the other. There is a good deal to say about this conflation of two very different mental activities; and a good deal hangs on it for an account of aesthetics. Given the time during which Saussure was working, it is understandable that he did not make the required distinction. However, its omission in the work of structuralists and their post-structuralist followers, signals a failure at the heart of that cluster of theories.

One commentator, concerned with developing semiology in the visual arts, is Norman Bryson. While Bryson is primarily concerned with painting, his argument is broader in its conception than that. It is particularly relevant to our evaluation of architectural aesthetics, since it holds such a strong position in the theory of visual art, taken broadly, and its understanding. We shall return in Chapter 10 to consider in more detail the significance of the philosophy of mind for these matters. For now, we should note that Bryson, in pursuing the semiological analysis of visual art, draws upon the philosophy of mind to support his argument. Identifying 'perceptualism' as his target, Bryson tells us that 'semiology approaches painting as a system of signs. The emphasis on *sign* may seem odd, but what this term in the first instance displaces is the term *perception*.'[13]

In developing his argument Bryson rehearses Wittgenstein's remarks on rule-following. In particular, Bryson wants to adopt Wittgenstein's rejection of the authority with which first-person perspectives are supposed to provide us with incorrigible self-knowledge. Bryson, takes two examples that Wittgenstein uses. The first is the self-ascription of understanding when we deem ourselves capable of calculating according to a formula. The second is when we ascribe to someone the ability to read.

> With mathematics, for example, I may have a vivid picture in my mind of a certain formula, but the criterion of my awareness that the picture was a *formula*, and not simply a tangle of numbers, would be my awareness of its mathematical application. The test of whether or not I had understood the formula would not consist in

the examination of my private mental field ... but in my executive *use* of the formula.[14]

Bryson, by enlisting Wittgenstein's conception of language meaning, believes himself able to provide an account of visual interpretation that turns its attention to the social context of the artefacts of visual culture in general.[15] In so doing the work of those involved in making visual artefacts becomes highly charged politically. It is not how the visual object looks – not what it is like for us to perceive the object – rather, it is the political significance of the object in a broader social context. The sections of the *Philosophical Investigations* that Bryson points us toward deal not only with meaning in language use; but also with our mental capacities and the mental concepts that we would have to employ to give an account of meaning. I do not think that Bryson has properly understood Wittgenstein on this set of highly controversial issues.[16] We shall return to them in Part III. For the moment we shall note that Bryson is attempting to give an instrumental account of the significance of visual artefacts. If our understanding of the meaning of visual artefacts is to be conceived along the lines of our understanding of language, then Wittgenstein offers much by way of support. 'For a *large* class of cases – though not all – in which we employ the word "meaning" it can be defined thus: the meaning of a word is its use in the language.'[17] In his notebooks which form the basis of the *Philosophical Investigations*, Wittgenstein is perhaps at his most clear. He considers the lure of thinking of the meaning of propositions as being immaterial mental items; and then goes on to show how inappropriate that would be. That is to say that the meaning cannot be a shadowy thing that is privately entertained by the mind:

> Without a sense, or without the thought, a proposition would be an utterly dead and trivial thing. And further it seems clear that no adding of inorganic signs can make the proposition live. And the conclusion that one draws from this is that what must be added to the dead signs in order to make a live proposition is something immaterial, with properties different from all mere signs.
> But if we had to name anything which is the life of the sign, we should have to say that it was its *use*.
> If the meaning of the sign (roughly, that which is of importance about the sign) is an image built up in our minds when we see or hear the sign, then first let us adopt the method we just described of replacing this mental image by some outward object seen, e.g. a

painted or modelled image. Then why should the written sign plus this painted image be alive if the written sign alone is dead? – In fact, as soon as you think of replacing the mental image by, say, a painted one, and as soon as the image thereby loses its occult character, it ceases to seem to impart any life to the sentence at all. (It was in fact just the occult character of the mental process which you needed for your purposes.)

The mistake we are liable to make could be expressed thus: We are looking for the use of the sign, but we look for it as though it were an object *co-existing* with the sign. (One of the reasons for this mistake is again that we are looking for a 'thing corresponding to a substantive.')[18]

Wittgenstein has Russell's conception of propositions in his sights in this section and throughout his considerable comments on language meaning. Russell had held that propositions are mind independent, language independent logical objects. That is to say that if a French sentence, 'Le pain est dans la cuisine', has the same meaning as the English sentence, 'The bread is in the kitchen'; then there must be something independent of each sentence and therefore each language that is 'the meaning' that each shares. And so propositions were held to have a shadowy existence. If Wittgenstein is right, then we should say that, given the 'life of the sign' is its *use*, then the fact that we use these sentences in similar circumstances either side of the English Channel, is what provides them with their equivalence. It is a point worth noting, and a point to which we shall return, that instead of thinking up 'occult' objects to secure the meaning of language, Wittgenstein goes *out* into the public realm; and finds there in the practices with which we are engaged the security of the meaning of the language we speak. That is to say that he sees language as intimately connected with, interwoven with, the whole circumstances of our lives.

The insistence on the notion of use and meaning is clearly welcome to those who, like Bryson, seek to move our attention away from the perceptual nature of visual culture, toward the role of the visual in the political context. That is to say, toward its active role in social contexts. But that is a move that pays too little attention to perception in the visual arts and to experience in the arts more broadly. Bryson is concerned to show that perception, being subjective (on his peculiar view), renders our understanding of art subjective. By contrast, recognition of the power of works of art relocates the seat of meaning. As he puts it:

STRUCTURALIST ACCOUNTS

A changeover from the account of painting in terms of perception to an account of painting as sign is nothing less than the relocation of painting within the field of power from which it had been excluded.[19]

And again,

The point is that mathematics and reading are activities of the sign, and that painting is, also.[20]

This appears to be a radically instrumental view of art, which holds no special place for experience in its account of our understanding or appreciation. However, if we took the view that the phenomenology of looking at visual artworks is not an essential part of them; if we treat them as signs along the lines of reading and mathematics, as Bryson supposes we should, then we would ignore that which is essential to our appreciation of the visual arts. Let us pursue this point.

Recent empirical work on perception might further support such a view. In neuroscience experiments have been carried out on the 'wiring' of frogs' visual apparatus to show that at least some functions of 'the visual' are treated only as signals and do not provide evidence of the frog's having undergone an experience. That is to say that there is evidence in these studies of frogs to show that some reactions to 'visual' stimuli do not have phenomenological presence in the frog. This persuasively supports the view that lower-order signals are in operation in 'blindsight' patients.

The evidence is this. Ganglion cells have been isolated within frogs' retinas, whose function is to trigger the tongue of the frog in capturing small insects. The route from the optic nerve of the frog is 're-wired' to the optic tectum in the opposite hemisphere of the frog's mid-brain. The result is that where an insect-like stimulus appears in the frog's vision the frog flicks its tongue to the exact mirror location within its environment in an attempt to capture the insect. However, its ability to negotiate boundaries within its visual environment is not impaired. This, we are to assume, shows that there are lower-order visual processes that do not register as appearances in the frog's phenomenological life. The frog hops along, negotiating its environment according to its visual perception of that environment – no doubt in search of some beautiful maiden whose kiss shall transform him into a handsome prince with all manner of opinions upon architecture; albeit one who cannot control his tongue.

Blindsight patients who have suffered lesions affecting their visual apparatus are often able to carry out tasks requiring the location of objects in their visual field. They are able to pick up objects without being able to describe their appearance or carry out precise manoeuvres such as catching objects whilst complaining of being totally blind. The objects picked up or caught do not appear to the subjects. These patients report that they cannot 'see' the objects that they otherwise react to in ways that exhibit sightedness. This is evidence for a lower-level operation within 'vision' which does not require representation; and which would appear to have no correlative phenomenology.

Vision, it is thought, has two aspects. One of these, present in human beings as well as other higher animals, is the representation of the world in terms of identifying objects and locating them spatially; the other is acting according to processed visual information where that is not necessarily processed representationally. This is an elementary aspect of vision from which we are to assume representation evolved.

This may seem an odd way to conceive of the arts. It is introduced here merely to support the view that phenomenology might be thought redundant in accounting for the significance of works of visual art.

> Vision evolved in animals not to enable them to 'see' the world, but to guide their movements through it. Indeed, the visual system of most animals, rather than being a general-purpose network dedicated to reconstructing the rather limited world in which they live, consists instead of a set of relatively independent input-output lines, or visuomotor 'modules' each of which is responsible for the visual control of a particular class of motor outputs.[21]

I do not know what Bryson and his colleagues would make of this; but if you imagine this piece transposed to the world of art and architectural theory, it reads almost like a manifesto piece for the politicization of art; and for deriding the aesthetic attitude. The question that such an empirical piece of research raises for our present concern is this: could it be possible to merely 'read off' the meaning of a work, in such a way that whatever it was like to look at it, that 'look' is superfluous to the meaning of the work and to our appreciation of it?

Imagine a special case of blindsight; one in which a spectator could read off the meaning of a work while having no phenomenological experience of its visual character. Would such a subject's grasp of the work be impoverished?

A good deal of what we have to say about this, however, will turn on whether we are really to think of meaning in the visual arts as being fashioned out of the same resources as we find in the use of language.

IV

At the level of theoretical discourse there is not much to be said in favour of structuralism and semiology. It is misconceived in ways which run at odds with the aims of the visual arts and aesthetics. Most of the critical insights delivered in its name, could be reformulated at little cost, with greater clarity, and with more persuasive power, were the reformulation to dispense with the cumbersome and technical jargon attempting to secure its position. We shall see, in Part III, how the shortcomings of structuralism distort and disfigure the conception of aesthetics in both contemporary art and architecture.

Nevertheless, the intellectualization of architecture along the lines informed by structuralism has been widespread. Concerned with meaning, the architectural theorist has had little to say about the nature of the aesthetic experience of architecture and, unsurprisingly, theory has tended toward establishing and sustaining 'meaning' and its interpretation in the works of architects. In consequence, architects have themselves cared less about aesthetic experience and focused more upon the meaning of their art. As a result of this, criticism directed at structuralism has been directed from within. Again, architectural theory has sought to benefit from applications of structuralism and its criticism from the other arts. We shall return to the tenets of structuralism and to consider how best they might be criticized from outwith the doctrine. Now, however, we must turn to the internal criticisms to see how they have connected themselves with the leading thinkers in architectural theory.

CHAPTER 6

POST-STRUCTURALISM

As long ago as Roland Barthes' essay, 'The Death of the Author', and his book, *S/Z*, structuralism loosened its claim to provide secure accounts of fixed meanings, in some cases inverting its previously held tenets, and paved the way for the emergence of post-structuralism.[1] Barthes, hitherto a protagonist of the structuralist analysis of all things cultural, conceived of the text as an independent structure that could be studied independently of any authorial intention. 'The Death of the Author' and *S/Z* straddle structuralism and post-structuralism, concerning themselves with the elimination of the author from the meanings of texts. That is all of a piece with the structuralist view that language is a system and can be studied scientifically and independently of any particular act of speech or writing. It also maintains the conception of a sign derived from Saussure and written into Barthes' *Elements of Semiology*.[2] However, given that the interpretation of works of literature calls upon specific readings of texts, the 'death of the author' signalled a turn against there being any one specific meaning, or 'closed' meaning, that a work would have. Structuralist analysis, that is, can no longer be expected to furnish us with *the* meaning. There are only readings.

In *Of Grammatology*, Derrida's extreme version of post-structuralist thought, the French philosopher positioned himself against the systematization of language meaning and became immensely influential not only upon artists, writers and theorists in general, but upon architects in particular.[3] Post-structuralism, along the lines of Derrida's thought, has come to be known as deconstruction. Derrida introduces the word *différance* as a play between the French word *différence*, meaning 'difference', and *déférence*, the act of deferring, postponing or putting off. Let us return to the idea of a lexicon; one that contains all the words in the English language. Supposing you want to know what the word 'pan' means. You can look it up in the dictionary, itself a kind of stipulative lexicon, and you will find a definition, say, 'a vessel of metal or earthenware'. Now you might wonder what the word 'metal' means, and so you would return to your dictionary to find, 'any member of the class of substances represented by gold, silver, copper'. And now you might wonder what the word 'substance' means and so on, *ad infinitum*. That is to say that every meaning is not only determined by the difference it has from other words in the lexicon; but that its meaning is always deferred until the other meanings in the lexicon are completed. But since every word in the lexicon awaits its meaning, we are constantly 'thrown back' in search for other meanings. The systematic relation between a word and the rest of the lexicon is a syntagmatic relation. The throwing back of meaning or the deferral of meaning is paradigmatic or associative. The influence upon architectural history and theory can be adduced from Adrian Forty's consideration of the term 'formal' as it appears in architectural discourse:

> As an adjective of 'form', 'formal' has all the complications of 'form' – and some more. 'Formal' is regularly used with the intention of giving emphasis to the specifically 'architectural' properties in works of architecture; but as the nouns with which it is generally linked – 'order', 'design', 'structure', 'vocabulary' – are themselves so ambiguous, the confusion is compounded.[4]

By emphasizing the associative or paradigmatic, Derrida inverts the priority of the two dimensions of meaning posited by Saussure. The free play of association permits puns and celebrates 'slippage'. We are no longer bound by the secure ties of meaning promised by structuralist analysis. Derrida, in terms familiar to the post-structuralists 'deconstructs' the framework which had been used by the structuralists to secure the location of meaning in language.

That is, of course, a caricature of Derrida's thought, which is always convoluted and complex, if sometimes entertaining. I rehearse it only to show that post-structuralist thought attacks structuralism from within. The post-structuralist, that is, conceives of the structuralist project as tainted by the search for fixed meanings. Accepting the notion of a sign, and of the nature of signs within the lexicon, the post-structuralist is able to use those notions to undermine the structuralist's ambitions and to show them to be insupportable given the foundations upon which they are supposed to rest. There are no fixed meanings. Meanings are always shifting and in a constant state of being propped up by other meanings, themselves in need of support. Post-structuralism is the English-speaking version of the theory we are considering. However, its French name is not so set in opposition to structuralism:

AESTHETICS AND ARCHITECTURE

Habermas's ... *The Philosophical Discourse of Modernity* ... was a violent critique of French 'neo-Structuralism' which contained a systematic refutation of Derrida's thought ... It is important to note that the term 'neo-Structuralism' never became current in English. What was preferred was 'post-Structuralism', a term also coined in the late 1970s in the wake of many 'posts' invented then (post-modernism was to appear more durably successful, although it too has lost its lustre). Let us imagine what might have happened if the British and Americans had been using 'neo-Structuralism' instead of 'post-Structuralism': instead of the forced inscription of history into the 'school' gathered by the -ism and the concomitant illusion of having superseded an older and exhausted movement, there would have been a sense of compromise ... In fact, the concepts of 'neo-Structuralism' and 'post-Structuralism' overlap almost completely; this can be verified by the roll-call of authors criticised by Habermas: after Nietzche and Heidegger, he names Derrida, Bataille, Foucault and Castoriades. In Habermas's account, nevertheless, it is Derrida who figures as the main suspect of a dangerously pervasive levelling of the 'genre distinction between Philosophy and Literature'.[5]

This passage weaves together two of the themes that we have been concerned with in this book. We have been trying to understand the relationship between structuralism and post-structuralism; and that has been viewed as a continuous, or at least an internal, development; so that post-structuralism can be seen as having inherited at least some of the intellectual commitments of its structuralist forebears. However, the last part of the quoted passage returns us to the position put forward in Chapter 4. Derrida, for whatever reason, erases the distinction between 'philosophy' and literature. Hence, in Derrida's thinking, truth is not necessarily the ambition of the pronouncements of post-structuralism.

That is not just to say that Derrida's anarchic attitude to authorship provides him with a radically relativistic view of meaning. The erasure of the difference between philosophy and literature encourages the collapse of the distinction between the search for truth and the pleasure of engaging in discourse more widely conceived. This way of conceiving the pursuit of post-structuralism permits the post-structuralist to escape the first move that might be made against him. The post-structuralist says: 'There are no truths'. His adversary then asks: 'And what am I to take that sentence to assert?' 'There are no truths' that is, embodies one half of the biconditional of the liar paradox. If it is true that there are no truths, then the sentence used in the assertion that there are no truths, is false. And, *ipso facto*, it cannot be held to be true. If, however, Derrida and those who follow him, work only for the pleasure of entering into discourse we need not take them as seriously as we might otherwise have thought required. That is to say we might find the writings of the deconstructionist interesting but unconvincing. Commitment to the 'truths' of deconstruction is not required of us, we might think. If this is a plausible reading of the post-structuralists it falls in with the view expressed earlier in Chapter 4, that we find these writings entering into the conception we have of the work as an aesthetic object, whatever we may think of the veracity of the writings concerned. So it is that Derrida collapses the distinction between literature and philosophy. We shall return to the idea that the practice of an art contains its theory, not as truth, but as a filter through which the work can be seen.

Using the playfulness of post-structuralist conceptions of language as a model upon which to envisage the visual arts, artists and architects have rebelled against the doctrines of modernism and sought to make works that incorporate ambiguity to a high degree and that would scandalize their stricter forebears. In architecture, for instance, the New York, New York Hotel in Las Vegas, is about as far away from our conception of a building constrained by the doctrines enshrined in modernism as any contemporary architect might wish to travel. That is a fine example of American post-modernism. More theoretically connected with post-structuralism (and in particular with the work of Derrida) is the French architect Bernard Tschumi. Tschumi's *Point de Folie*, a series of red objects (follies) scattered throughout the Parc de la Villette in Paris, is an attempt to make an architecture that is the 'deconstruction' of architecture.

The following is a quote from Bernard Tschumi to be found on a website dedicated to *Point de Folie*:

> Derrida . . . asked me why architects should be interested in his work, since, he observed, 'deconstruction is anti-form, anti-hierarchy, anti-structure – the opposite of all that architecture stands for.' 'Precisely for this reason,' was my response.[6]

What is it that Tschumi regards himself as opposing in architecture; so that it constitutes a counterpart to Derrida's opposition of hierarchy, structure and fixity? Derrida's position is to be seen as an inversion of structuralism and the various securities it had promised.

AESTHETICS AND ARCHITECTURE

4 New York, New York Hotel, Las Vegas (exterior)

POST-STRUCTURALISM

Tschumi is taking the proclamations of modernism and inverting those. If we look at Umberto Eco's attempt to provide architecture with a sense of meaning along structuralist lines, we will find the sorts of certainty that both Derrida and Tschumi rail against. Here is Eco writing on the nature of a sign, in this case the stairway, as part of the semiology of architecture:

> That a stair has obliged me to go up does not concern a theory of signification; but that occurring with certain formal characteristics that determine its nature as a *sign vehicle* (just as the verbal vehicle *stairs* occurs as an articulation of certain 'distinctive units'), the object communicates to me its possible function – this is a datum of culture, and can be established *independent of apparent*

5 'Greenwich Village', New York, New York Hotel, Las Vegas (interior)

behaviour, and even of a presumed mental reaction, on my part. In other words, the cultural context in which we live (and this is a model of culture that holds for several millennia of history as far as certain rather stable codes are concerned) there exists an architectural form that might be defined as 'an inclined progression of rigid horizontal surfaces upward in which the distance between successive surfaces in elevation, *r*, is set somewhere between 5 and 9 inches, in which the surfaces have a dimension in the direction of the progression in plan, *t*, set somewhere between 16 and 8 inches, and in which there is little or no distance between, or overlapping of, successive surfaces when projected orthographically on a horizontal plane, the sum total (of parts) falling somewhere between 17 and 48 degrees from horizontal'. (To this definition could of course be added the formula relating *r* to *t*.) And such a form *denotes* the *meaning* 'stair as a possibility of going up' on the basis of a code that I can work out and recognize as operative even if, in fact, no one is going up that stair at present and even though, in theory, no one might ever go up it again (even if stairs are never used again by anyone).[7]

Eco attempts to shoehorn architectural understanding into the all pervasive semiological framework. That is an extended quotation. I use it to show what kind of thinking Derrida and Tschumi were trying to overturn, from within the structuralist tradition. There are a number of observations we might make here. My dog, for instance, potters about the house and only ever uses the stairs to negotiate his passage between the floors. Does that mean that the 'cultural meaning' is engaged by my dog? Do we really work out that the stairs are a code? (I doubt I have thought about the stairs in my house in this way.) And poor Umberto Eco; he might have managed to get to the top of the house but he is forever stuck there, without any means of working out how to get back down.

It is with the idea that every cultural object must have some fixed meaning and that architecture must obey certain laws of construction and function that called for the inversion that Derrida and Tschumi sought to provide. Bernard Tschumi invited the architect Peter Eisenmann and Jacques Derrida to join him in putting proposals together for the competition at the Parc de la Villette. Derrida says this of his meeting with Eisenmann:

When I met Eisenmann, I thought in my naïveté that *discourse* would be my realm and that architecture 'properly speaking' –

places, spaces, drawing, the silent calculation, stones, the resistance of materials – would be his. Of course I was not so naïve; I knew that discourse and language did not count for nothing in the activity of architects and above all in Eisenmann's. I even had reason to believe that they had more importance than the architects themselves realized. But I did not understand to what extent, and above all in what way, his architecture confronted the very conditions of discourse, grammar and semantics.[8]

It remains unclear quite at what level the architecture (as opposed to Eisenmann's writings) is supposed to confront these linguistic conditions. The point of passing through this and other renditions of architectural thought and practice is to show how architectural theory, and in consequence architectural practice, has been caught up in philosophical discourse as to the nature of architectural meaning and its relation to the meaning found in the other arts. It is clear that the concentration on meaning, and in particular linguistic meaning, has distorted the nature of how it is that we might ordinarily think of our responses to the arts. It is only by removing the power of these high-blown theories that we can look afresh at the nature of the arts in general and consider more coolly how we might best profit from them. Before doing so, however, it is important to look at one major thinker from the English-speaking philosophical tradition who has, himself, persevered with a view that the arts in general can be best thought of as forms of language. We turn now to the work of Nelson Goodman.

CHAPTER 7

ARCHITECTURE AND SEMANTICS

I

In the last two chapters we have been looking at structuralism and post-structuralism and at the semiological analyses the former school uses in its presentation of meaning for all things cultural. Semiology, as we have seen, hopes to scientifically uncover the real meanings that lie beneath the supposed natural order of cultural artefacts. Semiotics, often used interchangeably with semiology, has a quite different origin. The semiotician, Charles Sanders Peirce, wanted to provide a much wider examination of the notion of a sign that is more akin to our notion of a signal. Thus it would include the passing of 'messages' between insects and even plant forms. In his work in semiotics, Peirce provides a taxonomy of sign systems, such that we can assign to any instance its place and function in the natural or linguistic world.

The American philosopher who has most rigorously attempted to apply semiotics to the understanding of art is Nelson Goodman. He has written extensively on the arts and sciences; and has had an enormous influence upon both philosophy of science and aesthetics. Across the arts Goodman has recommended that we regard their various instances as intrinsically linguistic.[1] In further addressing the particular arts, he published, 'How Buildings Mean', which applies his general theory to architecture. In particular, Goodman asks, what makes a building a work of architecture?[2] And his answer is: that it is a building which refers beyond itself, and thereby connects up with the world outside.

The structure of Goodman's argument is as follows. Language makes reference to the world. (Note the difference between such a conception of language and the project with which the structuralists and post-structuralists involved themselves.) The simplest and most common kind of reference is denotation. A word denotes by picking out some object or other in the world. The word 'Berlin' picks out, denotes, that city in eastern Germany, delimited by its established boundaries. 'Marilyn Monroe' picks out, denotes, the actress who

ARCHITECTURE AND SEMANTICS

played 'Sugar' in *Some Like it Hot*. Denotation connects bits of language to the world and is word → world directed. Now just as the name 'Marilyn Monroe' picks out that actress, so too does a portrait or a photograph of the same woman. So portraits and photographs denote their sitters. We read the name 'Marilyn Monroe' and, if we understand it, we are able to locate that bit of the world to which it refers. The name 'Berlin' denotes that eastern German city; but so too does the word 'city'; and so too does a picture postcard of Berlin; perhaps one that is a photograph of the Brandenburg Gate. All denote by referring to Berlin. We might put it: Berlin falls under the denoting piece of language, be that a proper name, a common noun, or a depiction. Not many buildings refer in this way; but Goodman provides us with an example. The Sydney Opera House, Jørn Utzon's modern building in Sydney Harbour, denotes, and thereby refers to sailboats; their sails billowing in the wind. To understand the Sydney Opera House is, therefore, to grasp the reference to sailboats made by the architect in his erection of the building. So, the building, in its reference to sailboats, satisfies the condition that a work of architecture is building plus reference.

Since few works of architecture are denotative in this way, we might wonder in what way other buildings secure their status as architectural works. How do they refer, if reference is the means by which instances of language, including all the arts, connect up with the world? In order to answer this question Goodman introduces the notion of exemplification.[3]

In exemplification, properties of objects are referred to by means of context. An object has an infinity of properties. Not all of its properties are, or could be, exemplified. Those properties that are exemplified, and thereby referred to, are those that the context (within which we observe the object) determine to be referential. His famous example of exemplification is a tailor's swatch. I go to my tailor and browse through his swatches. What am I doing? I am looking at a book of cloths, each different from another in some respect. They are alike in their size, their presentation, their pinking-sheared edge; and so on. However, they exemplify the (relative) weight of the cloth, the pattern, the weave, the colour, the tone and so on. Only those properties that are relevant to my consideration of the cloth, as a possible material from which to cut my suit, are exemplified. Exemplification is a form of reference that runs in the direction world → word. How does this apply to buildings?

Consider the modernist Arne Jacobsen's St Catherine's College Refectory, Oxford. That building is built on supporting beams,

6   Arne Jacobsen: St Catherine's College, Oxford (exterior detail)

which in turn support the flat roof. The walls of the building are curtain walls. That is to say that they do not support anything. In demonstrating the means of constructing the building; and thereby exhibiting some of the functional features of the building *qua* building, Jacobsen leaves a gap between the top of the curtain wall and the flat roof. This gap is then glazed. The glazed strip enables the spectator to understand how the building is constructed and how each element of the building contributes to the structure in its entirety. Each element of the building, then, exemplifies the role it plays in the building's construction. So, the building does not denote anything, in the manner in which the Sydney Opera House denotes sailboats. Rather, it exemplifies its means of construction; and in so doing, it refers to properties that it has *qua* building. In this way it satisfies Goodman's requirement that a work of architecture is a building plus reference.

Not all buildings exemplify their structures. Indeed, some buildings deliberately hide their construction. Baroque and rococo buildings are lavishly detailed in ways that provide visual effects which conceal or at least veil their material support. On a visit to Barcelona Cathedral with the architect Mike Guy, he commented that the columns in the Gothic interior looked like bunched curtains suspended from the roof, rather than as structural columns holding up that roof. In other words, if Mike Guy's imaginative appreciation is an appropriate response, the columns in Barcelona's cathedral militate against the exemplification of structure.

Goodman brings under exemplification a further means by which buildings refer. This subset of exemplification, he calls expression. Expression is a form of exemplification, but it is metaphorical, whereas straightforward exemplification is not. In exemplification a building refers to properties that it literally possesses. In expression, the building exemplifies properties that it does not, and probably could not, possess. The example he uses is of a Gothic cathedral which possesses, metaphorically, the property of 'soaring and singing'. Since no Gothic cathedral literally soars or sings, the building is said to exemplify these properties metaphorically. The

7   Arne Jacobsen: St Catherine's College, Oxford (interior detail)

building expresses the properties of soaring and singing. Barcelona Cathedral does not literally possess columns which are suspended from its roof; and so Mike Guy's suggestion (that the columns are to be understood as hanging from the ceiling) is to be seen as the building referring to its 'suspended' columns by means of expressing the property of suspension in what is literally its compressive means of support.

Finally, we are given an example of 'mediated reference', in which chains of reference are put in place so that by combinations of denotation, exemplification and expression, we come to see the building as referring to some part of the world or some quality or property to be found therein. The example he gives is of a church which *denotes* sailboats (presumably in something like the way in which Sydney Opera House denotes sailboats). Since sailboats *exemplify* freedom from the earth, which in turn *expresses* spirituality, the church is now deemed to refer to spirituality along this 'mediated' chain of reference.

One thing we can say straight off about Goodman's theory is that it is clear, precise and intelligible. It is straightforward in its conception of language as a referring system; and straightforward too in its setting down of how it is that the pathways of meaning in the arts are to be conceived. It does not sit easily with either structuralism or post-structuralism, other than that it is a theory designed to show how it is that language and reference provide the only resources we need to construct a theory of meaning for architecture.

As it stands, this theory excludes the spectator's experience of the building; or at any rate it pays no great attention to it. Since the occurrence of reference is concerned only with tracking the connections with, and thereby the location of, the object to which the referring term is directed, the presence or otherwise of an experience is of no importance. It is, therefore, difficult to see how we could come to *value* works of architecture, rather than merely understand them. Moreover, the value that we ascribe to works of art in general, is a value in the work of art itself; and not merely an instrumental value. We value the train timetable for the information that it gives up to us. We do not value it in and of itself. But how do we get from the correct reading of a work of architecture to its value? The hamburger-stand fabricated in fibreglass to look the shape and colour of a giant hamburger is, on Goodman's view, a work of architecture to stand with any other.

It is because we are concerned with the experience of art – and with the meaning of art only insofar as that enters into our experience – that we must forgo the claim of the theoretician that language provides a suitable model with which to compare our understanding of art. We return to this in Chapter 10, where we shall have to equip ourselves with tools from the philosophy of mind.

II

Goodman follows Peirce in his pragmatic interpretation of art and architecture. In this he can be thought to share at least some of the views that the post-structuralists hold with respect to 'fixity' of meaning. 'Some writing about architecture may give the impression that prose is as prominent an ingredient in architecture as steel and stone and cement.'[4] Indeed, the idea of 'the text' persisting through structuralism and its post-structuralist succession deliberately disregards the distinction between language and other cultural artefacts. Making cultural objects just is 'writing' – as we have observed in Barthes' 'writing the city'. In another place, Goodman seems to endorse such a view. On cross-modal variations – where a work in one mode of 'language', say music, is a variation upon another work in another mode, say painting, Goodman tells us that, 'variations upon a work, whether in the same or a different medium – and still more, sets of variations – are interpretations of the work; the Picasso variations function as much in this way as an illuminating essay on *Las Meninas*'.[5] Since, on Goodman's view, all art is language, it is hard to read this as anything other than the claim that an essay on *Las Meninas* or indeed any other work of art, is an interpretation of that work; and therefore achieves the same status as any work of art that alludes to another. Goodman is writing about David Alpher's series of pieces on *Las Meninas*. However, we might think here of Steven Holl's Stretto House, Dallas, Texas, which is cited as a translation of Bartok's *Music for Strings, Percussion and Celeste*. Whatever we might think of the plausibility of a work in one medium (or modality, to use Goodman's favoured terminology) being translated into another medium (being presented in another modality), the thought is that an essay can achieve the same status as a work of art. It does this by being an interpretation of the work it has as its reference.

However, we have no clear idea of what interpretation aims at, in the sense that Holl's Stretto House is an interpretation of Bartok's music. That is to say that we have no clear conception of what a 'faithful interpretation' would be, given that Holl is a creative artist making a work of his own. Similarly, we cannot have any clear idea of what a faithful interpretation of Velázquez's *Las Meninas* should look like, in order to assess the Picasso variations. Perhaps, then, we should simply think of variations as 'mere storytelling'. Presumably, the teller of the story takes the original and tells the story according to his lights; thereby making it a variation. The matter of faithfulness to the original then recedes in its importance. The interpretation, being a story, does not aim at truth.

As a matter of fact, I doubt that works can translate, in any strict sense. But it is clear that the descriptions we give of baroque architecture carry over into the realm of baroque music. And when we look across the arts, we see time and again the comparative similarities in which 'cross-modal' works are invested with significance. We think not only of the baroque, but of classicism and romanticism; and then more specifically of surrealism, minimalism, brutalism, realism, post-modernism and so on. The intellectual concerns of the artists, as these show up in the various works in the various modalities, form the filter through which we come to see the work under view. This, I take it, is of a piece with the line we pursued in Chapter 4; that theory is not to be seen as aiming at truth, but rather, as being contained within the work as a filter through which we come to understand the artist's motives, concerns and intentions.

Goodman, however, when discussing the interpretation of architecture is concerned to distance himself from the radical relativism he sees at the heart of 'deconstructionism'. The post-structuralist has rejected the idea of a correct interpretation; and Goodman's notion of interpretation similarly denies that we should aim at 'absolutism'. According to Goodman the deconstructionist claims that 'all interpretations are extraneous to the work, and the critic's function is to strip them off. A work means whatever it may be said to mean – or, in other words, it does not mean at all.'[6]

Goodman proposes a third way. Negotiating between the two poles – that the work means whatever the architect intended; and that the work means whatever can be said of it – Goodman recommends 'reconstructive relativism'. The third way takes 'deconstruction as a prelude to *re*construction'. In reconstructive relativism we recognize that some interpretations of a work are right, while others are not. There is not much more offered by way of illumination; but it looks as if the pragmatist in Goodman wants to stop short of offering interpretations that have truth as their target.

Since the view remains irredeemably vague, we shall postpone the development of our conception of interpretation until we have drawn upon resources in the philosophy of mind in Chapter 10.

However, before moving on to discuss the possibility of a political or social meaning of architecture, we might remember the question that Wittgenstein raises concerning our looking at a figure and giving the content of our experience as a description. The question is whether the descriptive content of our experience is an *interpretation* of the figure at which we look. Since architecture is a visual art, the nature of what we see and how we see it is pivotal to our understanding of what the appropriate response to a work would be like.

> Do I really see something different each time, or do I only interpret what I see in a different way? I am inclined to say the former. But why? – To interpret is to think, to do something; seeing is a state.
>
> Now it is easy to recognize cases in which we are *interpreting*. When we interpret we form hypotheses, which may prove false. – 'I am seeing this figure as . . .' can be verified as little as (or in the same sense as) 'I am seeing bright red'. So there is a similarity in the use of 'seeing' in the two contexts.[7]

CHAPTER 8

POLITICS AND THE SITUATIONIST INTERNATIONAL

I

The work of the Dutch structuralist Aldo van Eyck, as an architect concerned with anthropological matters, demonstrates how it is that architecture can be seen to address matters beyond the mere form and function of a building. That is to say that van Eyck sought to provide depth to the institution of architecture by relating its practice to an understanding of the social constitution of man. If we had thought of function in terms of warmth, shelter and security; or in terms of spaces to accommodate designated activities, then we had thought about it in too constricted and too transparent a way. Architecture, according to van Eyck, is much deeper than that. Van Eyck, in his studies of the Dogon people, had thought to establish the ways in which the patterns of life are to be mapped onto, so that they are designed into, the buildings and artefacts through which, and in which, those patterns of life are shaped. Whatever we might think of the hidden depths that structuralism is supposed to uncover, we should take note of the political and moral dimension that is injected into architecture through such a perspective.

That architecture should be seen to embrace such a broad range of concerns might seem at odds with our initial proposal that architecture should be regarded as a visual art; and that its works were to be considered as visual objects. Indeed we have seen that this social motivation is one reason that historians and theoreticians, those such as Norman Bryson, have turned away from the *visual* in the visual arts in favour of the sign. The political and moral dimensions of architecture do not seem to be something that one could literally see in a building. This is a point of some importance; and we shall have to return to discuss it in due course. For the present, however, we need to look at the ways in which political and moral considerations have infiltrated the conception we have of architecture.

POLITICS AND THE SITUATIONIST INTERNATIONAL

II

Intellectual developments in the humanities have been largely influenced by French thought. Structuralism, while having its origins in the work of the Swiss linguist, Ferdinand de Saussure, is largely a French product exported worldwide. The British, anti-intellectuals to a man, have recoiled from theory and fought shy of its insights, being naturally suspicious of anything that countermands common sense. (Indeed, in the position set out in Chapter 4, there is a whiff of scepticism toward theory that, while it is founded in philosophical reflection, remains anti-intellectual in its thrust.)

Existentialism in France, under the legacy of Jean-Paul Sartre, uneasily straddled the moral and political aspects of human life. What might be found of particular interest in existentialist thought, and which is particularly relevant to our enquiry, is its aesthetic dimension. Sartre, himself, was influenced by the nineteenth-century Danish theologian, Søren Kierkegaard. 'How can I be a Christian?' is the question that faced Kierkegaard. The answer to that question, given the context within which it was asked, required introspection. Kierkegaard raised that question of faith, given that he found himself in an increasingly secular world in which so-called Christians acted in ways which were little or nothing to do with what Kierkegaard conceived of as the Christian life.

> Kierkegaard is often described as the first existentialist . . . A melancholy and guilt ridden Christian, he devoted his considerable literary skills to the defence of faith, conceived as an ultimate and unfounded act of spiritual commitment. Truth, he argued, is truth *for me*, the idea for which I can live and die. And in his *Concluding Unscientific Postscript* (1846) he tried to show that individual existence is the sole ground of all legitimate thinking. I exist as a concrete and freely choosing agent: this alone is certain, and all truth is *subjectivity*. There can be no answer to the riddle of existence – to the question *why* I exist – except in the exercise of choice. And if a choice is to be truly mine it must be criterionless, ungrounded, a pure 'leap of faith' into the unknown. Hence I solve the riddle, and retain my freedom by an unjustified commitment.[1]

Kierkegaard, writing in nineteenth-century Berlin, did not respect the Sunday churchgoer, whom he regarded as acting out of custom and deference to the expected norm. Rather, the commitment to an authentic life – chosen rather than passively received, no matter how

AESTHETICS AND ARCHITECTURE

difficult it might be to sustain – was in itself a realization of faith. Kierkegaard wrote pseudonymously 'aesthetic' books, as well as more straightforward philosophical treatises. Sartre, in similar vein, wrote fully fledged philosophical works as well as plays and novels. In both cases, the fables of Kierkegaard and the literary works of Sartre further developed and fleshed out the more scholarly work.[2] It may well be for this reason that the philosophy of these thinkers is more accessible than had it remained solely in the realm of university philosophy. It is certainly true to say that Sartre's work, and perhaps Kierkegaard's work seen through the filter of Sartre, has left a deep impression upon those concerned with morality in and beyond the arts.

For Kierkegaard and for Sartre, our essence consists in our freedom. A stone or an animal are each a piece of the natural world; and each has its nature written into it. An animal, however, behaves; and it behaves as it does because of the kind of creature it is. It does not choose to behave in a certain way, or to live its life according to a commitment it has made. An animal follows a life laid out in front of it. Man, on the other hand, is born free; and he can exercise that freedom in choosing the life he shall lead. A lump of mineral can be studied so that it might give up its chemical structure. An animal can be cut into, in order to discover its genetic constitution. A man is no different. The animal and the man have their genetic material determined by nature. A man's life, however, is of a different stature. An animal's life is unfolded according to a pattern inscribed in its nature; not so a man's. A man's life is there to be chosen. It is, therefore, a problem for a man, but not for an animal, as to *how* he might live.

Sartre's disdain for the bourgeoisie is based on the assumption that its members have not committed themselves to live in a certain way; rather they have passively acquiesced in a life of numbing servitude. They collude in supporting a given set of artificial values; values that remove from the bourgeois consciousness any obligation to think and to act for itself. For Sartre and for Kierkegaard the notion of an authentic life, with its own conception of success, is to be valued in a manner that the life of a servile bureaucrat, for instance, is not. There may be a Romantic feel to this conception of human life and its worth, and no doubt this is what is so appealing about such a conception. Our task, however, is to understand how such thoughts might interweave with our conception of architecture.

Sartre's later work attempted to unite existentialism with Marxism. The collective act, the act in solidarity, permitted groups to act in accordance with collective choices in the face of repression by powers exerted by those whose authority is to be resisted. It is with the politicization of existentialism that we can begin to see how the notion of freedom might influence artists and architects; and persuade them to connect their work to the project of insurgency or, at least, civil disobedience. The artist as a worker, involved in challenging the established customs and 'bad faith' of a society, has both an existentialist and a Marxist flavour. Notwithstanding their criticism of both existentialism and Marxism, the situationists can be seen as belonging firmly within that tradition. Certainly their anticapitalist stance, if not their anarchic pronouncements, can be regarded as of a piece with existentialism and Marxism. The Situationist International has been influential on architectural thinking that is now gathered under the label, 'urbanism'. (It has influenced much else in modern culture, too. The slogans painted in graffiti, by the situationists and their student followers, on the walls of Paris before the riots were written into the lyrics that accompanied punk music in Britain and the United States.)

III

The Lettrist International comprised artists, poets and intellectuals connected with the Dada movement and largely banded together as a reaction to André Breton's iron-fisted grip on the surrealists. The group worked together and produced 29 issues of their magazine, *Potlatch*, the last of which was entitled 'Bulletin d'information de l'internationale situationiste'. The Situationist International formed around a number of characters, the most important of whom, for our purposes, are the French thinker, Guy Debord, the Danish artist, Asger Jorn, and the Belgian writer, Raoul Vaneigem. A 'constructed situation' was defined as 'a moment of life concretely and deliberately constructed by the collective organization of a unitary ambience and game of events'. Moments, in situationism as in existentialism, were to be seized. In 1967 Guy Debord wrote *The Society of the Spectacle* and Raoul Vaneigem wrote *The Revolution of Everyday Life*. They inherited from Marxism the theory of alienation; and from existentialism the idea of the importance of accepting responsibility for each moment in a life; and hence the importance of autonomy. These writings were enormously influential in the lead up to the May 1968 riots in Paris.

This may seem a long way from the aesthetics of architecture. It is not. We saw in the influence of structuralism on van Eyck, the turn in attention away from the mere appearance of the building to the underlying structures that buildings could share with the patterns of life of a people. The Situationist International wanted to transform the life of the everyday. To this end it developed two main strategies. These are the *dérive* and *détournement*. The *dérive* is supposed to replace work. Instead of working, the individual is to wander the streets of the city, turning into unknown places and finding there a form of life with which he can engage and into which he can be absorbed. The social encounter with strangers is to be encouraged. This can be in bars and cafés; in the markets and along the canals. The encounter with the unfamiliar is the key to the *dérive*. *Détournement* is designed to replace art. The 'method' is to use the art of the past and to appropriate it for the purposes of the Situationist International.

We have looked at the post-structuralists' influence on the work of Bernard Tschumi. The situationists too have had their influence.

> Traces of the situationist techniques can be found not only in Tschumi's theoretical projects but also in his realized plan for the Parc de la Villette in Paris. Tschumi explains the project in terms of schizophrenic dissociation and recombination of elements, but it could also be understood as a combination of *dérive* and *détournement*.[3]

The work of these thinkers was not always as fanciful as to be taken as an anarchist rant. In his *Society of the Spectacle*, Debord thought that the media would come to be the great driving force of the capitalist economy in the latter half of the twentieth century, just as the motor car had been in the first half of the century; and the railroads had been in the last half of the nineteenth. Debord and Vaneigem pronounced that capitalism had created 'pseudo-needs' to increase consumption. Modern capitalist society is a society of consumption; and production is given over to the manufacture of commodities. 'Having long been treated with the utmost contempt as a producer, the worker is now lavishly courted and seduced as a consumer.'[4]

There was little work done that could properly be regarded as urban design or architecture. However, the influence of the Situationist International is still in evidence in the architecture schools and in the work of architectural theoreticians who teach there. Asger Jorn – according to the art historian, T. J. Clark, the greatest painter of the 1950s – wrote, 'Architecture is the final point in the achievement of any artistic endeavour because the creation of architecture implies the construction of an environment and the establishment of a way of life'.[5] The *dérive* is a way of living in which we are urged to get to know our cities in ways that the bourgeois do not. It is, we might surmise, what Roland Barthes would describe as 'writing our city'. It is not with the intricacies of the theory that we need be concerned. Rather, we need to see that there are intellectual influences upon architectural thought that do not merely take the building as the locus of what the work might be. The manner in which we are supposed to go about our lives has been introduced so as to engage with the process of architectural design and its theory.

In Britain, Archigram came to the fore as a group of architects celebrating the new technologies, but rejecting the capitalist exploitation of them. While little or nothing of note has been built by the group, in 2002 they were awarded the Gold Medal of the Royal Institute of British Architects, arguably the world's highest accolade in the field of architecture, for their contribution to architecture. Their work can be seen as an attempt to use the new technologies as a way of discovering their creative potentialities. Archigram rejected modernist formalism. Of their number, the most interesting is David Greene. In one of his works, Greene considers a chair beside a stretch of water against which a fishing rod rests. On the chair is a portable television set and a sandwich box. None of the items in the photograph is 'lined up' or organized in a symmetrical way. Greene is opposing the formal organization of modernism by proposing a pragmatic way of pursuing life that uses technology, the television set, and is set around leisure rather than work, the *dérive*. Greene, in opposing modernism, sought to rid the world of a static notion of what constitutes architecture; replacing that notion or extending it to include systems of communication and methods of production. Systems of communication have enabled the reorganization of work and the places in which we carry out our labours – call-centres in India and other economic 'imperatives' that have sent the 'outsourcing' of manufactured goods to the cheap labour markets of the developing countries. Methods of production have brought such items as fish fingers, the plug-in air freshener, the television dinner and other such conveniences. These packages are the source of wonder for Greene, who notes the 'surreality' and the absurdity of their presence. The question for the artist and the architect alike is: how can we create works of art and architecture in a world in which such consumerism – itself a symptom of false consciousness or bad faith – is now the norm? Echoing Kierkegaard's question, the architect and the artist, each a maker of forms of life, asks: 'How can I make an authentic work in an age subservient to economic imperatives? '

Fortunately, we do not have to address that question. Ours is more humdrum. Nevertheless, in looking at what practising architects take to be the concerns with which they approach architecture, we can see that the focus of attention has not always remained on the building itself. There are other architects working whose concerns are not with the buildings that might be constructed from their designs. These have emerged from the schools in the latter half of the twentieth century. 'Paper architecture' consists in works which are put forward *as* works of architecture but which are never intended to be built; and indeed in most cases they could not be built. The view is that architecture can accommodate works where the thought contained in the work is of an architectural nature. I mention this as a mark of how far from the built form of an edifice architectural thought *can* stray, whilst, arguably, still being considered architecture. We shall return to the status of architectural work that does not consist in building in the chapter on architectural thinking, in Part III of this book.

In the next chapter we shall attempt to make sense of the variety of interesting theses we have been considering. We shall try to establish a platform upon which to measure the claims made by architects, theoreticians and those who would pronounce upon architecture. In this chapter we have seen how the practice and the theory have intertwined in ways that make for a complexity, unknown before the modern period. It is not merely coincidence that we can see the work of these recent architects as developing along lines similar to that in the visual fine arts. David Greene, for instance, is as close as we might think it possible to be to a 'conceptual architect' in his parallel social and moral concerns with those identified by the conceptual artists.[6]

CHAPTER 9

ARCHITECTURE AS PUBLIC ART

I

Architecture is an ancient discipline. It combines, if we are to believe what we are told, the science of building with the art of living. In this broad mix it exercises the professional with matters concerning engineering and affairs more close to human happiness – if only philosophy could tell us in what that might consist. It is with a conception of happiness that we found the situationists attempting to reorganize our lives in such a way that our art and our architecture would embed our moral and political values. We saw, in Chapter 8, that architecture affords such moral and political investment; and that our interest in architecture might be returned with profit from such investment. How, then, should we conceive of an art that has such public significance?

We have considered in Chapter 3 the nature of architecture as a problem-solving form of engineering. We considered two prominent conceptions of design that attend upon this division into engineering and art. The first of these sees architecture as a problem-solving discipline continuous with structural design. As such the architect works within the confines of materials and structures; and designs according to given need and available material properties. If any *aesthetic* consideration enters into his project it is at the level of 'economy of means' – rather as an elegantly argued proof in mathematics. The second sees engineering in the service of a higher art, with beauty as its aim and aesthetic response as its appropriate mode of apprehension. In this broader, more artistic conception, the work of architecture need not constrain itself within material matters alone. Engineering is required to furnish the substratum of the further artistic aim of architecture. Architecture, however, is guided by ideas which range far beyond the mere structure the engineer provides to support them.

In this chapter, we shall consider a more humble conception of architecture and we shall call upon recent developments in art to flesh out the general conception of what a new architecture might

AESTHETICS AND ARCHITECTURE

achieve. Before passing on to this, however, we need to make a few observations regarding art and its history from within philosophical aesthetics. We rehearsed in Chapter 2 the place that aesthetic reason occupies in an account of rational agency. It was Immanuel Kant whose philosophical framework brought a fully fledged aesthetics to the heart of philosophy. Kant saw his work as furnishing a complete account of the rational mind; and hence, of what it is for a human being to flourish. Each of the three kinds of reason – theoretical, practical and aesthetic – was to be distinguished by its aim. Theoretical reason is marked out by its pursuit of truth; practical reason by its pursuit of goodness; and aesthetic reason by its pursuit of beauty. Theoretical reason, properly employed, prompts us from beliefs about the way the world is, to new beliefs about that world. If our foundational beliefs are true and our reasoning sound then our concluding beliefs, to which we shall be impelled by reason alone, will also be true. In moral matters we are persuaded by our beliefs about the way the world is, to act in ways which will bring about valuable ends. Practical reasoning, judiciously pursued, will prompt us to act for the good. Aesthetic experiences (at least one class of them) are the result of engaging in critical or aesthetic reasoning. In the case of dependent beauty, such an experience is a delight in an object seen as appropriate or fitting to its purpose. Thus we are to think of such an object as beautiful; albeit dependent upon the concept of the perfection of the object entering our judgement.

Architecture, like painting and sculpture, is a dependent beauty. It is not a mere composition of shapes, colours, solids and voids. Kant again:

> The beauty of a human being ... or the beauty of a horse or of a building (such as a church, palace, armoury, or summer house) does presuppose the concept of the purpose that determines what the thing is [meant] to be, and hence a concept of its perfection, and so it is merely adherent beauty.[1]

And again:

> In architecture the main concern is what use is to be made of the artistic object, and this use is a condition to which the aesthetic ideas are confined.[2]

Formalism, at least as that doctrine was promoted by Greenberg in the United States of America, misinterprets Kant's formalist view of free beauty. It does so by applying Kant's conception of free beauty to those realms that Kant shows to be dependent beauties. Greenberg applies Kant's formalism to painting. So presumably Greenberg would, or at least could, consistently consider sculpture and architecture as free beauties. By transposition we could look at sculpture as if it were the composition of three-dimensional shapes independent of any representational character. And we could look at architecture as a combination of volume and material independent of its having a character marked by its possible habitation. Taking my lead from Kant's conception of dependent beauty, as opposed to the lead taken by Greenberg from Kant's conception of free beauty, we must enquire further into the nature of aesthetic response when this is constrained by a concept of the purpose of the thing we are to judge.

Architecture, to return to the thought expressed at the beginning of this chapter, has been practised by some, as the art of living. Its responsibility, we might think, is to embed or enshrine common values that bind us one to another. These values include the respect in which we hold each other. So architecture, conceived as a public art involves a conception of ourselves as agents in a moral world. Just how we conceive of our freedom and how we conceive of the relations that hold between us will place constraints upon the way that we organize and design the buildings in which those relations are embedded. That is why we considered Aldo van Eyck's structuralist architecture. It is also why, in Chapter 2, we looked at contractualism, which we considered ethically sceptical, and placed that beside Kant's more optimistic and universal conception of morality constrained by reason.

If architecture is to be recognized as the place at which aesthetics and ethics converge, it is important that we seek to locate its value in the context of moral as well as aesthetic reflection. Its works provide the environment within which we see out the compass of our lives. In architecture, we feel the presence of our ancestors as well as that of our progeny. We feel bound not only to the communal present but also to the community beyond the present; that of our fellows brought alive in the art and architecture we have inherited; and of those who will live with us in the art and architecture we bequeath.

Architecture, perhaps now more than ever, has a duty to preserve and to sanctify our presence on this earth. This is not to champion conservatism at the expense of creativity. Far from it. One artistic value is originality. We want architects of whatever stripe to be inventive in their work. The history of art is full of invention and creative ingenuity. The inventive architect, placing himself in an

AESTHETICS AND ARCHITECTURE

historical context, is best placed to make comment on, and to add to, the work which he inherits and which constitutes his ground. We might say that it is only after a thorough immersion in the historical context of architecture that an architect is in a position to make inventive contributions to that living tradition.

II

The moment of modernism is past, we are to believe. Kant, as we have seen, was more than anyone else responsible for aesthetic modernism. One of the legacies we have from Kant is the notion of artistic genius. The artistic genius is the one who, following no rule, creates innovative art that provides the rule for others to follow. Nature speaks through the artist, and when it does so, we are rewarded by originality. Originality is the mark of genius. Here is Kant on genius:

> Genius is the talent for producing something for which no determinate rule can be given, not a predisposition consisting of a skill for something that can be learned by following some rule or other; hence the foremost property of genius must be originality.[3]

However he goes on:

> Since nonsense too can be original, the products of genius must also be models, i.e., they must be exemplary; hence, though they do not themselves arise through imitation, they must serve others for this, i.e., as a standard or rule by which to judge.[4]

The cult of genius in modernism, some fear, has had a ruinous effect upon the art and architecture of our age. I leave it to others to judge which works of contemporary art are (and which ones are not) worth taking as standards for the study of art and architecture; and for its critical development.

What is heartening at present is that there is a sea change in the ways in which many artists are conceiving of the work with which they are engaged. The public art movement has seen many talented artists eschewing the pursuit of personal expression in favour of works that celebrate communities. Works by sculptors such as Ed Allington, Tom Lomax, Tess Jaray, Antony Gormley, Richard Wilson, David Mach, John Aiken and Rachel Whiteread, all testify to the emergence of an art that is considerate of a public and sensitive to its variety of values. These artists could not have produced the work they have without concerning themselves with the particular publics for whom the works were made. Here the shift from the artist as genius – living on the periphery of society, a misunderstood outcast from the central values of that society – to the conception of the artist as someone who makes a work responsive to the conditions of a community and to its history, and to its values could not be greater. It is with this kind of sensitivity to the communities, for whom these works of public art are made, that I wish to return to the conception of architecture.

Architecture just is a public art. Its works are placed in public spaces and together they form our towns and our cities. Art, when it went public, had to address the issues arising from its newly found publicity. Architecture has always been public. Public artists, I have no doubt, have looked to architecture to learn the methods of public consultation, negotiation, development and constraint. Architecture should involve its public at this very broad level. The client for architecture must be conceived more broadly than just the funding patron. The client, so conceived, and for whom both architect and patron are responsible, is the community whose use of the building has to be considered. (I take it for granted that walking past a building or seeing it next to another is, in some relevant sense, to use the building. In which case, all who live in and use the city are to be considered within the client group.)

Innovation and invention are required by newly formed social needs. The modern world is woven together by historical threads that bring races and religions together to form a vibrant and colourful social fabric. We want our artists and architects to make works which respect the community at large and which draw upon our shared respect for partial histories. (Those histories, as partial as they may be, have brought us together in our shared condition.) In architecture we want buildings that encourage the community to come together. I think that Will Alsop's Peckham Library is such a project, whereas the vastly overrated works of Zaha Hadid and Daniel Libeskind are really just legacies of the old idea of the modernist genius. A library is a good place to start. So is a house, a bar, a church, a museum, a stadium and, perhaps most strikingly of all, a monument. This is where people come together to share their lives. These are the sites of congregations.

Conceived as accessory or as conditioned, beauty brings with it the idea of perfection, as Kant calls it. When we consider the concept under which a work of art is fabricated we immediately grasp the criteria by which we *can* judge experiences. Also, we can see how the moral and aesthetic come together. A building can engender what Wittgenstein called a 'form of life'. The form of life will be that of a community whose values are to be found in the use of the building in which it finds its home; where members of the community live and love and laugh and labour. Architecture, as all the other fine arts, finds its worth in the ways in which it provides a common sense of who we are. These can be more or less stable; sometimes confirming our deep sense of community; sometimes leading us to recognize new and more cohesive ways of living together as a series of communities in search of common values. So experience, the aim of aesthetic reasoning, can be seen to result from critical argument.

Let us conclude this chapter with consideration of a particular monument: the Washington Vietnam Veterans' Memorial. Monuments, in general, provide a striking example because their function is only minimally defined. However, a monument – being the thing that it is – constrains our aesthetic response in just the same way that a building's being a library constrains our appreciation of it. I have chosen the monument for a second reason. The monument seems to lie at the intersection of architecture and public art. So that if public art has anything to teach architecture, and vice versa, then the monument should prove a fertile site for the focus of our present concerns.

At the time of its commission in 1982 the artist, Maya Ying Lin, was an undergraduate architectural student at Yale University. There was an inevitable outcry from the reactionary quarter who wanted a more 'traditional' public monument to those who lost their lives in the Vietnam War and the veterans who served in it. Sited just a few metres from Ying Lin's black-granite 'Wall' is Frederick Hart's bronze sculpture of three American soldiers. We now look at these two responses to the loss of life suffered by 58,000 American soldiers in the Vietnam War.

> After someone has died we see his life in a conciliatory light. His life appears to us with outlines softened by a haze. There was no softening for *him* though, his life was jagged and incomplete. For him there was no reconciliation; his life is naked and wretched.[5]

This quote from Wittgenstein is meant to show us something about both those who have survived and those who have died. It shows us something of the relationship between the living and the dead. If it has explanatory power in general, then that power is concentrated in our thoughts both of and for the war dead. For these are lives cut short – 'jagged and incomplete'. Maya Ying Lin's wall brings the solemnity of that particular thought home to us. It does so in a number of subtle ways that are worth rehearsing here.

The vastness of the black wall containing all the names of those who fell brings home the enormity of the loss to two generations of Americans. The gradual descent as visitors pass along the wall is like the sinking of a ship. The visitor feels himself submerging into the darkness of the grave. The name of each soldier is sought by relatives brought here to mourn their loss. The highly reflective surface of the black granite reflects the visitor as he looks at the name of his lost relative. The stark contrast of standing in the light below the level of the ground, looking into the darkness and seeing the name of a relative, while seeing one's own reflection in the granite brings home this contrast of the absent (merely named) and the present (seen in reflection). The inscribed granite reminds us of the headstone of a grave, yet this is no ordinary grave, for it is a headstone for each of the 58,000. (Again the enormity of the loss is brought home to us.) The gutter between the granite wall and the promenade is filled with flowers lain at the foot of the column that bears the name of a lost soldier. Visitors, that is, have come to treat this wall as a shrine for their dead. (One of the overall most moving characteristics of attending the monument was, for me, the silence that it demanded and received from all who visited and passed through in respectful procession.)

If the enormity of the loss strikes us when we focus our attention upon the monument, Ying Lin never loses sight of the fact that each of those 58,000 soldiers had a name which individuated him or her. So we are reminded that the enormous sum was made up of single lives. (This, of course, was an important political motive for fighting that particular war in the first place.) As the visitor searches for the single name of his lost relative, we are reminded of the importance of the individual.

No cry of torment can be greater than the cry of one man.
Or again, *no* torment can be greater than what a single human being may suffer.
A man is capable of infinite torment therefore, and so too he can stand in need of infinite help.[6]

If any work of art were called upon to do justice to this insight from Wittgenstein, then I believe that Ying Lin's work could be appropriately cited.

The most important feature of this work is that it actively engages the visitor. He comes into a lived relation with American history in his visit. There is a ritual demand for a certain kind of reaction to the work. It is not merely the distracted spectatorship that visitors have to statues of dignitaries in some town square. The work operates with the viewer, so that in his place in the procession he becomes part of the work.

By comparison, of the three soldiers as they figure as a tribute to 'those who served', there is very little that can be said that connects the sculpture to the dignity of our memorial thoughts. It seems such a feeble effort compared with the magnificence of the black wall. The power of Ying Lin's work surrounds one. The visitor inhabits the piece and cannot do other than reflect upon the nature of war and loss.

In this it operates at an architectural level as public art. We learn from this example that architecture has the power to frame our lives and embed our values and beliefs. The strength of Ying Lin's work is that it shapes our experiences by engaging our disposition to project both thought and emotion onto our perceptions. It says what it says so quietly and calls upon our quiet and restrained attitude toward it. Architecture can do this by providing us with places in which we feel the beauty and fragility of our dignity together with the solemnity of the lives that we lead within its embrace. It can bring together the different strands of a multicultural society. Not by representing their differences, but by uniting those different communities into one. It does this with a startling originality which at the same time calls upon all manner of established human reactions; human reactions that transcend racial and social differences. Respect for our fellows, even in the face of the solemn recognition of our human condition, is one path that we might follow in the hope of finding human happiness.

Concerned with the art of living well, and sensitive to community needs, we might develop architecture in ways which allow us to celebrate originality. It remains for us to guard against original nonsense.[7]

We turn now to consider what responses we bring to the various theoretical positions that we have been considering in this part of the book.

PART III

ARCHITECTURE IN MIND

CHAPTER 10

THE MIND AND ITS FURNITURE: A PHILOSOPHICAL RESPONSE TO THEORY

I

In the first two parts of this book we have been looking at various attempts to provide an account of architecture. Several views have been put forward and their various positive attractions and motivations have been taken into account. Notwithstanding the admirable motives with which these theories have been pursued, the theories fall short of answering our question with any degree of satisfaction. We need to see why those theories fail and then we need to put in their place a broader account that will accommodate a view of the value that we invest in architecture and its many works. We are now at a point at which we need to call upon additional resources if we are to make headway with our task. It is time to consider developments in the philosophy of mind; so that we might be in a better position to assess the views we have been dealing with so far.

To be sure, the second part of this book has moved in the direction of the reception of architecture. It has had to take into account the fact that in understanding architecture we have to reflect upon its place in our lives. The nature of architecture that we seek to explicate, that is, concerns more than consideration of features of mere buildings – the works as physical objects out there in the environment. In three of the chapters in this second part of the book, we looked at a series of proposals that sought to deal with architecture as a language. We now need an account of mind in order to be able to properly assess those views. This chapter then comprises two strands. It aims to demonstrate the shortcomings of the language views; and at the same time it aims to provide a platform upon which to build a positive account of architectural understanding.

II

Thankfully, we shall leave aside a good deal of what currently exercises philosophers who work in philosophy of mind. We shall not be concerned with the fundamental questions as to what constitutes a mind, although we shall be considering at least some of the mind's constituents; nor shall we be visited by such perplexing questions as to what the precise relationship is that holds between mind and brain (or mind and body; or mind and central nervous system). Rather we shall be concerned with what we might call mental terminology. What are we to make of such things as concepts, perceptions and beliefs? What is imagination; and what is its role in aesthetic understanding? In a word, we shall be concerned with at least some of the furniture of the mind. What is the right way of conceiving the various features of mind that we invoke when thinking about architecture and its proper reception?

Our study shall centre on the mind insofar as getting clear about certain mental phenomena will help us to elucidate the nature of aesthetic appreciation as that is to be found in our dealings with works of architecture. To an extent, we have encountered this already, as when claims were made concerning the nature of our linguistic capacities and how they are engaged in our apprehension of architectural meaning. In particular, Norman Bryson enlisted the help of Wittgenstein in his attempt to rebut one version of what Bryson has dubbed 'perceptualism'. Also, we found Goodman's reconstructive relativism too vague as an account of architectural interpretation. Let us then look at a range of mental phenomena as they have been used in discussing the arts in general, and consider their implications for a theory of architecture.

The mind and its contents might seem mysterious. But we can begin by reviewing fairly clear features of some of the phenomena involved. We start our study with a distinction. Not everything in or connected to the mind need appear in consciousness. That is to say that some features of the mental realm do not require any presentation to our conscious states in their explication. However, by contrast, some features of the mind are *essentially* present to consciousness. Let us begin by considering propositional attitudes. Mental attributes exhibiting the structure of propositional attitudes are among those facets of the mind that need not make an appearance in consciousness. Propositional attitudes are characterized as attitudes an agent takes up toward a proposition. A proposition, loosely speaking is a structured thought, where the structure of the thought is captured in the grammatical form of a declarative sentence or assertion.[1] (I am using 'thought' here in a neutral sense in which both conscious and non-conscious states of mind can be captured by the concept.) Propositional attitudes are those attitudes we take up toward such propositions. 'I believe that . . .', 'I hope that . . .', 'I fear that . . .' and so on. We can conceive of propositional attitudes being taken up by someone who is not conscious of them; and indeed, by someone who might never become conscious of them. Propositional attitudes encompass, among others: beliefs, hopes, fears, desires, intentions and knowledge. Such propositional attitudes are captured by attributing to the holder a disposition to act in a certain way. If I hope for a letter from my friend; I shall be disposed to listen for the tread of the postman as he nears my front door; I shall hang on after my normal departure time in case I might catch the post, and so on. If I am afraid that the faculty provost has heard I have been making fun of his blue shiny shoes with brass trimmings, I shall be disposed to avoid the places in which he is normally to be found lurking. If I believe that the bus leaves for the station at 16:50, I shall be disposed to arrange my affairs so as to arrive at the bus stop at 16:45.

Many of my intentions never appear to me. It might take some effort to get me to recognize an intention I had, even if the intention is fulfilled – as Freud has shown us. Even where I deliberate and come to formulate a plan, the consciousness of the formation of the intention is not essential to it. It is not an essential feature of dispositions to act that they appear to consciousness. In large part, they remain dormant; to be acted upon when the relevant circumstances obtain. There are many things I believe, including beliefs I have of which I am unaware; many hopes and fears, intentions and desires, that never present themselves for inspection via introspection. The upshot of this is that where my attitude toward a particular proposition is brought before my consciousness, its meaning cannot be located there. If, for the sake of a philosophical exercise, I bring before my mind the belief that Paris is south of London, that proposition cannot have, as part of its meaning, my awareness of it. For the belief is the same belief I had before calling it up as an example in the exercise.

My consciousness would be in a pretty unmanageable and chaotic state, were all my propositional attitudes to be present to it, over the duration of my waking life. My mind would be swamped, were I to hold in front of it the plethora of propositional attitudes I have adopted. As a general rule, the propositional attitudes I have do not enter my consciousness. I believe, for instance, that Queens Park Rangers beat West Bromwich Albion by three goals to two in the 1967 Football League Cup Final. It is a belief I have held *continuously* since the day they won the match back in 1967. One might put it, rather oddly but accurately, that since the game *I have been disposed, should the occasion arise, to affirm the proposition that* Queens Park Rangers won the League Cup in 1967.

Compare this to the itch on my left wrist where my wristwatch has irritated it. The itch is present to my consciousness; and indeed the itch lasts just so long as I am aware of it. Itches, pains, smells, tastes, colours and sounds are presented to me by my sensory apparatus by way of my central nervous system including my brain. It makes no sense to say that I have an itch but that I cannot feel it. And the 'feel' that we talk about here is the presence of sensation in consciousness. There is something it is like to undergo sensations. They have a phenomenology.[2] Propositional attitudes, which are not intrinsically phenomenological (indeed, as we have just seen, they are rarely presented to consciousness), continue through our sleeping as well as our waking moments. It is true of me, that if I am hoping for a letter from my friend, and that if I am afraid of the faculty provost's reaction to my spitefulness, then my hope and my fear persist through my sleeping moments. I do not cease to believe that Queens Park Rangers won the League Cup when I go to sleep at night. That particular belief, while properly attributable to me, is not something that can be given a precise duration. Sensations, by contrast, have a definitely determined life, the duration of which is given by the precise amount of time they occupy my consciousness.

Unasserted beliefs have been held by all of us without our ever having been aware of them. We all believe, I presume, that there are no six-legged mauve giraffes native to north London. Indeed the presentation to my consciousness of six-legged mauve giraffes – which I occasionally 'see' on my short journey from The Duchess public house in north London's Holloway Road to my nearby home – is evidence, not for a change of belief, but for an overdue change in direction of swing for the '*bibulum pendulum*'.

The structures that comprise our propositional attitudes accommodate concepts we have mastered. Beliefs, as it were, are constructed out of our conceptual stock in order to fit the world as we find it. Concepts, then, like those beliefs in which they find themselves employed, are not intrinsically present to consciousness. Like beliefs I hold, there are many concepts that I have of which I remain unaware. Mastery of a concept is demonstrated by my using the concept in some way that is congruent with its logical shape, so to speak; by its appropriate deployment in a propositional attitude or in the expression of such a proposition; or in some other way acted upon in the engagement of a disposition. There is no phenomenological description that is necessary in order to master a concept or to hold a belief. It is plausible and indeed often the case that while we are all familiar with a concept, it is difficult to pull out of it just what individuates it as that concept. Knowledge is of the same order. There is nothing it is like to know that gold has the atomic number 79. And, as with beliefs and concepts, there are many things I know of which I remain unaware.

III

Sensations, experiences and imaginings, however, are all of them constituted by their presentation to consciousness. We shall have something to say about differences between them later. For now, however, we can hive this group of mental features from that group of attributes in which we have penned beliefs, concepts, intentions and knowledge. This group of mental phenomena *necessarily* appear to consciousness; it is an intrinsic feature of sensation, experience and imagination, that they have a phenomenology. Whereas for propositional attitudes – belief, hope, fear, intention and knowledge – they need not. It would seem, then, that propositional attitudes are not sensitive to whether or not they are conscious states. Whereas the group of experiential states we have mentioned have consciousness as an essential feature.

Sensations are the raw feels that we have in virtue of the fact that we are sensitive to certain sorts of stimuli. I am sensitive to colour, to sound, to tastes and smells; and to the relative resistance of surfaces as they come into contact with my body. These sensations result from the various ways in which features of foreign objects intrude upon me and irritate my sensory system. It is on this basis that sensations ground experiences. Our experiences are constructed out of the sensations we receive via our sensory apparatus and our internal nervous system.

Now, in discussing mind, we seem to have two independent ways of accessing its content. For sensations, it looks as if we had best refer to the person undergoing the experience. If, suddenly, everything appears warm and red to me, then I seem to be the sole authority upon the matter. I have the last word. That is because in speaking of sensations we are not dealing with the phenomenon of intentionality.[3] Relatively speaking, I can have sensations that are independent of the environment in which I am situated. Moreover, pleasures seem to be just as radically subjective. The pleasure that I take in a warm bath is not about anything. It is simply a sensation enjoyed.

If, however, I hold the belief that the bus leaves at 16:50, then the belief has implications for the way that I am likely to act as a result of having the belief, hurrying for the bus stop so as to be there by 16:45. We might be inclined to think, then, that sensations and the other experiential cluster of mental phenomena, being essentially present to consciousness, are best accessed through first-person perspectives. Whereas the attribution of propositional attitudes, being non-sensitive to states of consciousness and effecting events in the public realm, are best accessed by the third-person perspective. All phenomenological *states* are accessible only to the first-person perspective. They are incorrigible. All propositional attitudes are accessible, in principle, to the third-person perspective. Propositional attitudes, unlike phenomenological states, are submissive to correction; they are corrigible. This does not deny that I can know of an animal's pain by observing its behaviour, nor that via introspection I might come to know about what it is that I have certain hopes and fears. Rather, it says that the two different perspectives offer independent epistemological routes to the mental phenomena we have been discussing. And that those mental phenomena with an essential and distinctive phenomenology favour the first-personal perspective, while those which are characterized by their taking up a propositional attitude favour the third-person point of view.

This is not to say that we cannot attribute simple non-intentional experiences to persons in the grip of sensations. If I see a person holding his jaw and moaning, I can quite confidently attribute toothache to him; or if I hear the moans of pleasure from someone surrounded by chocolate wrappers, I can attribute gustatory pleasure to him. Nevertheless, the person undergoing the sensation remains the final authority upon his states. Since undergoing sensations essentially involves consciousness, it is reasonable to assume that a person has immediate access to them. In taking the third-person perspective upon the attribution of propositional attitudes, we heed the thought that some attitudes do not show up in the consciousness of the person whose attitudes they are. Moreover, propositional attitudes hang together in the complex network of a person's mental life. In this way we regard them as rationally assessable. The arrangement of my affairs such that I am to be at the bus stop for 16:45 involves not only beliefs, but also hopes, desires and intentions in a network of complex relations. This is not the case with sensations. We regard a primitive organism, so long as it is deemed to be sentient, as capable of undergoing sensations. We do not, however, consider such forms of life as adopting propositional attitudes.

This may seem remote and removed from the world of architecture. My aim is to build up a view of our mental life such that we can locate and describe aesthetic response in general; and then go on to reflect upon the nature of aesthetics as that permeates our understanding of architecture. It is important, therefore, to show that experience belongs to a different mental category than does belief and knowledge. We need to discriminate between these mental phenomena in order to be able to draw out their interconnections in perception. So that we can then go on to deliberate upon the perception of architecture and the special kind of experience involved in our understanding of architectural works.

IV

Since perception is a means of acquiring knowledge, we need to say something about the relation between how things look to a subject and how things are in the world. We need to see how it is that the look of things provides the subject with access to that world. In doing that we can show that the character of how things look, while having subjective qualities – colour, smell, taste, sound, texture – can, nevertheless, provide objective knowledge. We thereby provide an account of how our subjective states reach out to the world beyond.

To this end, we should notice that perceptions enjoy both sets of characteristics of the mental phenomena that we have discussed so far. That is to say, there is something it is like to perceive something – perception essentially involves a phenomenology – and that in representing the world, perception is conceptually structured; and is thus constitutive of the propositional attitudes that we take up toward the world represented. This is, after a fashion, to rehearse the Kantian view we sketched in Chapter 2.

We can think of perceptions, then, as compound mental states made up of sensations *and* propositional attitudes. Recalling the nature of each of these mental characteristics, we can see that the propositional attitude can outlast the experience. Thus, I can draw on perception to form belief. The belief that I have as a result of my having perceived that 'there is a woman sitting in front of a window that looks onto the Sussex Downs' is the perception that 'there is a woman sitting in front of a window that looks onto the Sussex Downs', shorn of its phenomenological aspect.[4] Perceptions, then, are alive in our formation of many beliefs and much of our knowledge. As such, perception is a cognitive feature of our mental life. Perception puts us in touch with the world beyond; and in so doing it structures that world according to the conceptual abilities we have developed and which we are able to deploy them.

As it stands, this will not do. For even if we have a structured perception of the kind that combines a phenomenology with a propositional attitude, we have not yet explained how it is that the world beyond enters our minds. To explain how it is that the subjective quality of perception provides a means of obtaining cognitive contact with the world beyond, we need to say something about how world and mind are related.

V

Perceptions, conceived as compounds of mental states, admit of two aspects. And this double feature of perceptions is captured in the dual character of the language we use to describe them. For instance, I can say, 'I see a woman sitting in front of an open window looking out on to the Sussex Downs'. I can also say, 'I see *that* a woman *is* sitting in front of an open window and *that* she *is* looking out on to the Sussex Downs'. The first of these locutions does not give structure to the perception in the way that the second locution does. That is to say that the first locution identifies the *object* of the perception – out there in the external world. The second locution provides us with the *content* of the perception – how the external world 'looks' to the perceiver; how the world is represented to him. It is with this second aspect that we have just been dealing in the last section of this chapter.

This double aspect of perception accords with our intuitions regarding the nature of our grasp of the external world. Perception is particular in that in its exercise only particulars can show up; and yet their showing up needs to be given in terms of general features. The causal theory of perception renders this intelligible. My seeing the woman in front of the window is caused by *that* woman sitting in front of *that* window. The woman's being in front of the window is the *object* of perception. The *content* of my perception is given in terms of observational concepts, that there is *a* woman with *such and such* a bearing with *such and such* hair in *such and such* light conditions and so on and so on. That is to say that these concepts enter into the propositional attitude engaged in the perception I undergo.

THE MIND AND ITS FURNITURE

To help us get clear about this distinction we might consider the attribution of perceptions to an animal. I can say of a cat, 'It sees the mouse hiding under the sofa'. But can I say, 'It sees *that* the mouse *is* hiding under the sofa'? The first locution attributes a perceptual state to the cat. The second locution, however, attributes perceptual content to what it is the cat perceives. Unless we have good reason for thinking that the cat has the concept of 'a mouse', 'a sofa' and of 'hiding', we ought to be reluctant to make any such attribution.

Objects in the world act upon us and arouse in us perceptual states that combine a phenomenological state and a propositional attitude. These objects are what we see; and we see them because of the effect of light as it is reflected from the object and intrudes upon our senses. (I shall remain focused on seeing, but the principles can easily be transposed to the other sense modalities.) How we represent the world out there is a matter of our apprehension. We apprehend the world as it intrudes upon our senses by taking up an attitude toward a content structured by the observational concepts we have to hand. Thus our perceptions contain something like a judgement. The world, so to speak, appears to me in perception, representationally.

Earlier in this chapter we mentioned the subjectivity of simple pleasures. Since these pleasures were characterized as merely sensational they were regarded as non-intentional. The pleasures were not about anything. However, in coming to understand the nature of a compound mental state such as perception, we can think of complex pleasures which are themselves compounds. Thus I can think of the pleasure I take in a work of art as being both essentially present to consciousness *and* being constituted by propositional thought. I take pleasure in the way an architect has organized an entrance so that upon entering the building there is a sense of greeting that is framed by a vestibule; there is a 'pause' built into the processional route that takes me from the embrace of the entrance into the building where I shall eventually prosecute my day's commerce.

My pleasure in this feature of the building is both imaginative and perceptual. I am not merely organized by the building. Rather, I take the building as an appropriate place to accommodate my sense of propriety. The vestibule is a place for momentary rest during the transition from my arrival at the building to my pursuit of the project with which I am engaged. The building, then, becomes a way of lending dignity to the human world of commerce.

VI

Imaginative experience, by contrast to perception, is non-epistemic. I cannot learn anything about the world by scrutiny of the content of my imaginings. Imagining does not bring the world into view in the way that perceiving does. Nevertheless, there is something it is like to undergo an imagining. In imagining something, a person can be more or less in the grip of an experience as of the object or scene imagined. By contrast to mere supposition, I take imagining to be a form of holding a mental image, visual or in some other mode of perceptual form, in front of one's mind. For the visual arts, the image attaches itself or fixes upon the perceived work. And so there is a relation between that which appears to the spectator and that which he imaginatively attaches to it. As far back as Aristotle we can find:

> That imagination is not the same as perception is clear from the following arguments. (i) Perception is either a potentiality or an activity, as, for instance, are sight and seeing, yet there are appearances in the absence of either of these, such as the appearances in sleep. (ii) Perception is, but imagination is not, always present ... (iii) While perceivings are always veridical, imaginings are for the most part false ... (v) Visions appear even to those whose eyes are shut.[5]

Aristotle did not make the distinctions that we have made and was unable, therefore, to accommodate misperceptions, as when the propositional attitude I combine with the phenomenological character of the experience turns out to be false. (There is something out there in the world that I see; and it is in the right way causally connected with my seeing it; but my propositional attitude provides me with an erroneous representation – I take a pile of rags to be an old man asleep in the corner.) Nevertheless, Aristotle's intuition is right. Perception puts us in contact with that which is present in our environments, whereas imagination calls to mind that which is absent. It is for this reason that we cannot imagine something that is presented to us in perception. As Wittgenstein puts it:

> [Mental] images tell us nothing, either right or wrong, about the external world. (Images are not hallucinations, nor yet fancies) While I am looking at an object I cannot imagine it.[6]

THE MIND AND ITS FURNITURE

We cannot learn anything about the world by scrutinizing our mental images. It is for this reason that we must treat the free play of imagination as an aspect of our mental lives that is disengaged from the processes with which we negotiate our environment. If I imagine that *p*, there are no conclusions that can be drawn from *p*. Whereas, if I perceive that *p*, I am justified in forming the belief that *p*; and from the belief that *p*, I can begin to make rational connections with other beliefs, desires and mental states in the process of negotiating the world as it appears to me.

Mental images have a phenomenology that they share, to some degree, with perception. There is something it is like to undergo an imagining. And visual imaginings have a visual character, notwithstanding the fact that they do not engage with our perceptual apparatus. Both perception and imagination are essentially present to consciousness.[7] My imaginings can have a structured content in much the same way that perceptions can. That is to say that imaginings, like perceptions, can combine a phenomenology and a propositional attitude. I can imagine that I am on the Mediterranean coast, bathed in sunlight and sitting by the lapping waters, sipping manzanilla and eating freshly grilled sardines. Imaginative experience of this kind, unlike perception, involves a phenomenology independent of the appearance of objects or scenes in our environment. Some imaginative experiences, however, are based upon present perceptions of the immediate environment. This is the case with at least some of the visual arts.

It is on the basis of looking at a representational painting that I come to have an imaginative experience as of the pictorial content. The present piece of coloured canvas is the object of my perception. It is on the basis of that perceived object that I am able to imagine a landscape, for instance.

> [Depiction] consists in seeing expanses of colour in such a way that, whilst remaining expanses of colour for one, they simultaneously in a special imaginative sense *bring a landscape into view*.[8]

While this remains a controversial view – or, at least, a view that has its opponents as well as its adherents – it is of a piece with the thrust of the argument being put forward in this book.

A further feature that differentiates imagination from perception is that imagination is subject to the will, whereas perception is not. I cannot, ordinarily speaking, refuse to see what is straight in front of my open eyes. My seeing is caused by what is in front of my eyes.

However, imaginings do not have the same causal history as perceptions. I can call up an image and I can banish it. Again we read in Wittgenstein,

> The concept of imaging is rather like one of doing than of receiving. Imagining might be called a creative act. (And is of course so called.)[9]

> If one says 'Imagination has to do with the will' then the same connection is meant as with the sentence 'Imaging has nothing to do with observation'.[10]

In this passage we see, again, the relation between imagination, the will, and the dislocation of imagination from the processing machinery of cognition (if I might allude to Kant's 'manifold of perception'). But we must now return to O'Shaughnessy's conception of depiction. For in his neat description of the phenomenology of looking at pictures we note that imagination can be fastened to perception. Thus far we have said little about experience. That is because the concept is extremely plastic. Such diverse phenomena as having a toothache and 'seeing' regret in the eyes of a portrait, count as experiences. And yet it is possible for a dog to suffer toothache. Dogs, dolphins and dragonflies, however, are unable to 'see' regret in the eyes of a portrait. (I wonder if dragonflies suffer anything so mean as toothache.) What is the difference between these two examples of experience? It is surely not one of degree. They seem to be experiences of different kinds.

That is why O'Shaughnessy describes the experience of looking at a picture as seeing the paint marks while a landscape *in a special imaginative sense* is brought into view. Some experiences we have involve perceptions upon which we can base imaginative experience. This does not contravene Wittgenstein's claim that when we are looking at something we cannot imagine it. For the imagined content of a picture is absent from us. What we perceive, that which is present to us, is the marked up surface of the picture. The imaginative *experience* is as of the content, which is not present to us.

So, in depiction, for example, we can have imaginative experiences which are as of objects or scenes absent to us, but which are given to us on the basis of perceptions of special objects present to us; in this case the marked surface. The deployment of ambiguous figures in the literature, in both psychology and the philosophy of mind, provide us with examples of how it is that an experience can change while the perception of the figure upon which the experience is based remains stable. In the example of the duck/rabbit ambiguous figure, nothing in my visual perception has changed while the change in the nature of the experience, brought about by the aspect change, takes place.

The change of aspect. 'But surely you would say that the picture is altogether different now!'

But what is different: my impression? my point of view? – Can I say? I *describe* the alteration like a perception; quite as if the object had altered before my eyes.[11]

We are not concerned with depiction here. However, the example is introduced so as to point to a feature of experience that we shall call upon in due course. The general feature is that of imaginative experience grounded in, or riding on, or fastened to, a present perception.

With these resources to hand, we are now in a position to assess the views that have been discussed in the second part of the book. What are we to make of the various attempts to assign meaning to works of architecture on the model of linguistic meaning? It is now time to lend dignity to those views.

CHAPTER 11

ARCHITECTURE, MIND AND LANGUAGE

I

The problems inherent in structuralism are inherited from Saussure's conception of the nature of a sign. We noted earlier that the sign unites the signifier and the signified but that the latter is a concept and not the referent. So, for instance, the sign, 'tree' unites the sound pattern and the concept *tree*; and so there is no particular tree to which this sign refers. This overall picture of language leaves out of consideration word–world relations. This, however, presents a problem for the structuralist account. Since it is a cornerstone of the theory, we need to know what the status of a concept is in this context. Saussure's notion of a concept or 'the signified' is not at all clear. It seems he is committed to the view that a concept is a mental entity; and that entity is represented ambiguously in the diagram he gives us.[1]

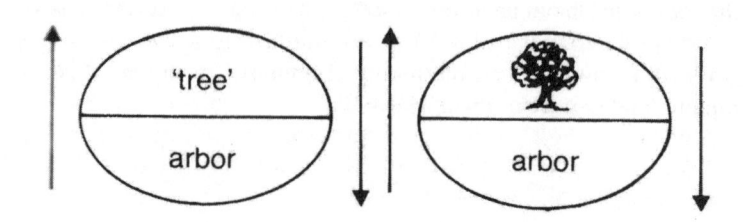

On the one hand it appears to be an image, and on the other, something else. Images, as we have seen, make poor candidates for the meanings attached to language. It is a feature of our having images that they occupy our attention. That is not so with the mastery of concepts. It is clear, however, that according to Saussure the signified is part of a psychological complex whole. John Sturrock, in his illuminating book, thinks that structuralists have often wavered between thinking of the signified as a concept and thinking of it as the object to which a word directly refers. He says that:

Grave misunderstandings of the nature of Structuralism follow if signifieds and referents are taken to be synonymous, as they are at one point in the text of the *Course in General Linguistics*, where one can read that 'the signified *ox* has as its signifier "boeuf" on one side of the frontier, but "ochs" on the other side.' This misstatement of the case, which contradicts the very terminology Saussure has himself introduced, is typical of many similar ones made since by others.[2]

Sturrock observes that there is a tendency to idealize the signified, so that we might come to think of it as existing separately from its signifier. There are problems for thinking of signifieds in these terms. For one thing it is hard to know how we could come to have a pre-linguistic concept; or what it would be to recognize one, for that matter. If we must take 'ox' to be the marker of some pre-linguistic mental entity which becomes a sign when united with a signifier in the shape of 'ox', 'ochs' or 'boeuf', then it is difficult to understand how the concept can be identified independently of a particular language. When whole thoughts, or the sentences expressing them, are considered, we would have to think of these thoughts as having a common meaning. That has something of the ring of a proposition, where 'propositions' were introduced to provide sameness of meaning across languages. We considered this in Chapter 5. If 'il pleut' means the same as 'it's raining', the thought goes, then there must be some meaning, independent of either French or English that is captured by both sentences.

On the view of propositional attitudes spelt out earlier in this chapter, we are able to think of the equivalence in terms of the attitudes that the French have toward the proposition 'il pleut' and the attitude the English have to 'it's raining'. Each has an attitude that provides him with a disposition to act in a certain way. I hand an umbrella to my wife, Vanessa, as she heads for the front door, saying, 'It's raining'. Jean-Paul hands an umbrella to his wife, Véronique, as she heads for the front door and says, 'Il pleut'. We do not have to think of propositions as being shadowy mental entities, made up of shadowy components that are non-linguistic concepts. Rather we can think of language as operational in the ways in which we lead our lives. The place that 'it's raining' has in my operational life is similar to the place 'il pleut' has in Jean-Paul's. That is where the equivalence is to be found; in our social operations, in the way we live.

If we turn away from the concept as a pre-linguistic mental entity awaiting its shape in some particular language we shall find problems with the notion of a mental image too. For my concept 'tree' does not have any attendant image; and even if it did, this would not be sufficient for the image to be granted the status of meaning. If my concept 'tree' is a mental image, then what does that mental image 'look' like? What sort of tree is the object of my mental image? Is it a fig, or an oak, perhaps? Or is it something between the two? The problem of correlating concepts with mental images is familiar to analytical philosophers from the work of the early empiricists; and in particular this can be found in the argument between Locke and Berkeley with regard to abstract ideas.

Locke had argued that our grasp of general concepts is acquired by collecting together all the instances of experiences of particulars. We then form a general idea by erasing detail as that finds itself in conflict between instances of particulars. So, my general concept of a man is not one of an old man or a young man, a black man or a white man, a tall man or a short man. Berkeley, taking ideas to be mental images complains that my idea of a triangle is a mental image of a triangle, and therefore itself a triangle. (If it is an image of a triangle it is a triangle.) Since all triangles are either scalene or isosceles it follows that I am not permitted to have a mental image of a triangle that is either. That, claims Berkeley, is absurd. It would mean that I have a mental image of a triangle (which is itself a triangle) but that this triangle is neither scalene nor isosceles. This did not prove what Berkeley wanted it to prove. The reason being that general concepts, abstract ideas, are not mental images; and a mental image of a triangle is not itself a triangle.

The view that ideas or concepts are mental entities or have experiential content has suffered a sustained attack, notably in the work of Wittgenstein, but more recently in the work of Hilary Putnam.[3] Both Wittgenstein and Putnam are concerned to connect concepts, and our mastery of them, with the public nature of the lives we lead. Both attempt to establish the nature of reference in such a way that we can understand how it is that language connects up to the world. So, for these thinkers the connection with the world is important in a way that it was not for Saussure. Nevertheless, the connections, when established, secure language *meaning* out there in publicly observable events and states of affairs. For both thinkers the mental entities – those to which Saussure attributed the locus of meaning – drop out of consideration; and so we see a response from analytical philosophy to a problem inherited from structuralist linguistics.

According to Putnam, nothing in the mental state I undergo when thinking can guarantee connection with its content. He provides a number of examples to show how thought and world can come apart. Imagine that I am dreaming and that in my dream I am in a room with another and a great weight is about to drop on his head. In my dream I shout at my companion to warn him of the danger. My shouting in my dream is correlated with my shouting in my sleep and my shout awakens me. I find myself in a room just like the room in my dream; and I find that a great weight is about to fall upon my companion's head. My shouting in my sleep has alerted him to the danger and he moves so as to avoid the falling weight. This is marvellous luck; but just because it is luck shows that his being alerted to the danger is not something for which I can take credit. I shouted in my sleep. There is no standardly correct connection between my psychological state and the real events in the room. So, while the internal 'look' of my mental state has the same content as if I had been awake, there is no route from how things seem to me to how things are.

Putnam imagines a case where a man has undergone hypnosis. The subject has no concept of trees. He believes, wrongly, that he speaks fluent Japanese. He has a stream of Japanese phonetic sound patterns flowing through his mind, all of which, by some fluke, are identical with perfectly formed Japanese sentences about trees. Images, as of trees, are present to him while the 'discourse' flows. Still, the man is not referring to trees and on waking the man will realize that he did not really know what was going through his mind while under hypnosis, even if it seemed to him that he understood it at the time. A description of what was going on in his head at the time will be qualitatively identical with that which would have gone through the mind of a competent Japanese speaker when he talks of trees and thereby refers to them. No connection between the hypnotized subject and his language competence is in place. From this we are to conclude that neither mental words nor mental images intrinsically refer. For a description of language competence we have to look to the public realm, in which language competence has to meet the demands of the language speaking community.

If we move to the place that language has in our lives, we get a picture of the practical nature of the connection between language and the world. There are entrance rules and exit rules that take us from experiences into discourse and lead us from discourse out into action. It is the intimate connection between our talk of objects and our non-verbal transactions with them that provides reference to our utterances; and hence connects language with the world in a way that demonstrates the *use* of language. I refer to apples, not because of some magical link between a mental picture of an apple and an apple; but because in talking of apples or imagining them, I rehearse the ability to buy them by weight, to eat them, to throw them at people, or simply to look at them in some still-life arrangement. Over and above seeing them or imagining them, I know how to act with an apple.

It follows that reference to the world and its occupants involves the conception of entering into causal interaction with that world. Introspection of mental presentations will not yield any insight into what meaning is. The attribution of concepts to ourselves as well as to others is carried out by testing to see if we can suitably discriminate according to a concept. We shall need to see if we can act in ways that best exhibit the possession of a concept; and so on. In other words, concept attribution is essentially public. The inner presentations which we may have and which might appear to us to express our thoughts are only acceptable if they can be systematically linked up with other concepts and expressed in a manner that is publicly intelligible. Concepts are *signs in use*. They are, perhaps it might sound strange, abilities. Meanings are to be located in the social structure and not in the head. Mental content is only admissible as meaningful when this is converted into public form. This passage shows that Saussure was wrong to locate (associative) meaning 'in the brain'. That there are associations does not establish meaning; so much as depend upon it. Meaning is public in the first place; and private associations remain beyond the scope of meaning; to be enjoyed or discarded according to private wants and self-indulgencies.

If we now take up the thought that understanding language requires no attendant inner experience we come to see another feature of Saussure's model of language. Saussure had insisted, and correctly so, that our ability to discern phonemic structures requires of us that we recognize units of meaning such that they are reiterable. This is a recognitional capacity and so it is based in perception. However, Saussure does not distinguish the need to recognize perceptible chunks of *arbitrary* language, from examples of *experiences* imbued with significance, where the perception is not an arbitrary matter, but is the seat of such significance. This needs further explanation. However, it is worth looking at Saussure's description of the two dimensions along which he posits meaning:

> Syntagmatic relations hold *in praesentia*. They hold between two or more terms co-present in a sequence. Associative relations, on the contrary, hold *in absentia*. They hold between terms constituting a mnemonic group.

Considered from these two points of view, a linguistic unit may be compared to a single part of a building, e.g. a column. A column is related in a certain way to the architrave it supports. This disposition, involving two units co-present in space, is comparable to a syntagmatic relation. On the other hand, if the column is Doric, it will evoke mental comparison with the other architectural orders (Ionic, Corinthian, etc.), which are not in this instance spatially co-present. This relation is associative.[4]

Saussure connects the kinds of experience we have when looking at a building to the kind of experience we have when listening to another speak. However, the importance of the recognitional capacity in each case is of a different order. When I listen to another speaking, telling me which train I must join to get to London, for instance, it is important that I hear him and important that the noises he makes are distinguishable as recognizable reiterated patterns of sound which carry meaning. However, my interest in what he says is not *in* the sound patterns, but rather it is in the information that the words convey. It is an interest in the connection between the meaning of the words and the kind of action which they will lead me to take, running for the train, for instance. No intrinsic interest attaches to the sounds themselves. The case where I am looking at a building and I recognize the Doric columns, regarding this as a fine example of a Greek temple, or lamenting the clumsiness of the façade composition, is of a different character. Here my interest is in the *experience* I derive from looking at the building.

In the architectural case the oppositions between the Doric and the Ionic, or between Doric and the Corinthian, is an important feature of the experience of the building. The spectator's informed experience is enjoyable and intelligible at one and the same time. Here we might want to say that it is the experience he grasps in understanding the building upon which he looks. In the case where I find out which train I am to take, it is something of import that my recognitional capacities makes available to me. I pass through the experience of the language to its content and the relevance of that content for my immediate actions. The experience drops out of consideration, so to speak. It does not require my attention in the way that understanding the building does.

It is because we are concerned with the experience of works of architecture – and with the meaning of architecture only insofar as that enters into our experience – that we must forgo the structuralists' claims that language provides a suitable model with which to compare our understanding of architecture.[5]

In focusing upon the experience of architecture, we are able to better account for the complexity and richness to be found therein. We look at a building, say a classical temple in the Doric order, and in looking at it we consider its appearance in light of the Corinthian and Ionic orders. That is to say that, given our acquaintance with these other orders, we are in a position to have an experience of the temple at which we look. We consider its modesty and elegance, given that the Doric order provides a sparer, more solemn, encounter with the building. It makes sense to regard this as the content of the experience of *this* building, only if we can think of it in comparison with the Corinthian and Ionic orders. Those comparative thoughts, as it were, enter into our experience of the Doric temple. The richness of the experience has this propositional content folded into it, so to speak. But in giving the content of experience in propositional terms, we do not venture further than the experience. We recall here, that in providing propositional content for perceptions, we nevertheless insisted that the compound mental state had to have a phenomenology attached. Strip the perception of its phenomenological content and the mental state disappears, surviving, at best, as belief, which, as we have seen, is a mental disposition and so not a mental state.

II

Norman Bryson's account of semiology and visual interpretation interestingly called upon Wittgensteinian ideas in the philosophy of mind. However, Bryson too quickly draws conclusions from Wittgenstein's assessment of our grasp of language. He then proceeds without warrant to apply those findings to the nature of experience as that has been put forward in what Bryson calls, the 'perceptualist accounts'. Bryson is concerned with representation and with a refutation of the view that representational painting is supposed to duplicate the painter's perceptual field, where Bryson thinks of the perceptual field as a private inner experience. Bryson calls for *recognition* to replace *perception*. Recognition is supposed to give the viewer access to the meaning of the painting via social codes. That is to say that the look of the painting drops out of consideration in favour of a reading of the canvas.

ARCHITECTURE, MIND AND LANGUAGE

The point is that mathematics and reading are activities of the sign, and that painting is, also. My ability to recognise [a pictorial] image neither involves, *nor makes necessary inference towards*, the isolated perceptual field of the [pictorial] image's creator. It is, rather, an ability which presupposes competence within social, that is, socially constructed, codes of recognition. And the crucial difference between the term 'perception' and the term 'recognition' is that the latter is *social*. It takes one person to experience a sensation, it takes (at least) two to recognize a sign.[6]

We have rehearsed, in this chapter, the distinction to be made between the object of perception and the content of perception. We also noted that the causal theory of perception affords us a view of how it is that the mind and the world are connected one with the other. Perception, that is, while having a subjective feel, also aims at an objective content. Perceptions, in this sense, are not at all private. When we argue as to which horse crossed the line first; or about whether Thierry Henry's winning goal for Arsenal was offside, we are not comparing isolated perceptual fields, but rather we are arguing, on the basis of what we have *seen*, which horse came first, or whether the goal should have stood.

The reason that this is particularly relevant for our discussion concerning architecture is that Bryson wants to rid our understanding of experiential content. On Bryson's view, transposed to architecture, we would have to read off the social meaning of a building and we would not be permitted to call upon the content of the experience as a way of properly responding to the importance of the work. Bryson's view of semiology is that it replaces the role of experience in our aesthetic response with the intellectual achievement of reading in an ideological apprehension of 'power relations'. Bryson, *et al.*, remove aesthetic value from architecture and identify our responses to it as only instrumentally valuable.

When we first encountered Bryson's fusion of semiology and philosophy of mind, we considered there the notion of an animal, a frog, for whom responses to visual stimuli could be processed without recourse to phenomenological characteristics. The frog, we are to assume, simply responds to stimuli on the basis that its eyes collect information and process it without there being a 'what it's like' for the frog. And at the end of Chapter 5 we asked whether a spectator suffering from a peculiar form of blindsight would have an impoverished conception of architecture if he could respond to it by the use of his eyes, could become acquainted with its intellectual content, but could not *see* the building at which he looked?

It looks as if Bryson would have to answer 'No' to that question. On the view expressed here, however, we can answer that his appreciation would be diminished; and for the very good reason that our rehearsed view of perception permits the way things look to us to have contents which are permeable by thought; and which are enjoyable just because they are permeated by thought. So, we have done enough to establish the dependence of imaginative experience upon perception for representational painting. In so doing we have made a space for imaginative experience to occupy in our appreciation of architecture. Since architecture, like representational painting, is a visual art, we can maintain that perception is essential to our apprehension of its works. Blindsighted spectators are in the unfortunate position of being unable to see works of architecture, despite their ability to wander around and through them; and, as a result of their disability, they are unable to appreciate the buildings in which they falter.

III

We turn now to post-structuralism. Much of what flows from structuralism, including Derrida's deconstruction of it, has failed to give due weight to the experiential feature of our apprehension of meaning in architecture and the arts more broadly. Derrida inverts the relation of syntagm and paradigm, regarding associative relations as primary and using the neological concept of *différance* to show that the syntagmatic structure is always in need of something further to secure meaning.

However, the view of language that we have been developing here, in light of Wittgenstein's philosophy of mind, sees meaning as tied to the lives of a people. Language is, as Wittgenstein would say, 'a form of life'. That we can study languages as whole systems independent of their actual uses is an abstraction away from the life of the language. That is not to say that there are no important insights to be gained by the study of language as an abstract system; but it is to say that all such insights must ultimately return to the conception of language as reliable; albeit an ad hoc, piecemeal and pragmatic feature of everyday human custom and practice. For this reason we should turn away from the teachings of Saussure, as they have been interpreted and developed by the structuralists. But we have also seen that language secures its meaning – it does not fix it – in the social structures which are themselves abstractions away from the customs and practices in which we lead our lives.

Consider, for instance, the practice of sending letters and postcards to our friends and relatives. I write down an address on the envelope. I fix to the envelope a stamp which bears the price I have paid in order to contract the services of the Post Office. I then put the envelope in a box for collection, where I expect the letter to be taken to a sorting office. At the sorting office it is transferred to another sorting office that will place the letter in a post round. From there it is carried by the postman and delivered to the address I have put on the front of the envelope. There is quite a bit that can go wrong in this complicated and attenuated procedure. That is to say the letter might not reach my friend next day, when I might confidently have expected the letter to have arrived. What might we say about this?

My confident expectation is founded upon the reliability of the postal service through its long and successful history. However, that things might go wrong means that there is no guarantee that the procedure that I trust and in which I feel confident, will have the outcome I desire. Generally speaking, however, even where things go wrong, the letter will eventually turn up at my friend's address. Perhaps the sorting office placed the letter in the wrong post round. If that were so, it is highly likely that the postman would notice and return the letter to the office for its re-assignment; or if the address is similar to one to which the letter gets wrongly delivered, we might expect the recipient of the letter to put it back in a collection box so that the letter can be processed over again. The point is that, even where there is a failure of the proper process by which a letter gets to its intended destination, we have the means to redress the mistake and make good the expectation that the letter will be delivered. Moreover, it is the overwhelming success of the postal service that encourages us to use it as a means of sending and receiving messages. If it was less reliable, to any great degree, we would no longer use the system. The system would collapse. Is it not the same with language? We cannot guarantee that we shall be understood when using language. However, the overall success of language as a means of forming and exchanging ideas encourages us to use it. And again, where there is a failure of the language in our attempts at communication, we try to make other routes available to the recipient; or we correct each others language in order that mistakes that we make do not set us wrong. Of course, we make puns and we play with language and otherwise enjoy its accidental features and its ambiguities. But that is as a result of its being a successful means of communication; and not as an example of how it cannot be said to secure meaning.

In architecture, the expectations we have are similar to those we encounter watching football or listening to music. Our understanding is constrained within a practice; and we enjoy that practice when we are confirmed in our expectations, feeling gratified that our understanding had led us there in advance, as it were, of the game's unfolding or in the musical passage. Or, where the play or the music interrupts our expectations we are thrilled by the way in which the inventiveness of the football player or the composer has set us up to knock us down. We marvel at the ingenuity. This seems to provide a more realistic account of what it is like to regard a piece of architecture born out of the 'post-structuralist' movement. When we look at Bernard Tschumi's isolated follies in Parc de la Villette, we see them as inversions of our expectations, as refusals to make good the modernist promise of easy intelligibility. But it is not the intelligibility of language of which we are deprived.

Whether or not Tschumi's works are successful does not depend upon the truth of Derrida's post-structuralist enthusiasms. Rather, it depends upon the works being invested with our interest in them. This can, of course, be heightened by our appreciation of Tschumi's attraction to the language model, as seen through the lens of post-structuralism; and so post-structuralism gets into the experience we have of the follies. But, having entered our experience, it does not need to stand the test of truth, nor yet that of coherence, in order to make its presence felt. That Tschumi believes the assertions of post-structuralism enters our experience of the buildings; and it does so in a way that illuminates the experience we have of them. We are not, thereby, committed to the truth or otherwise of the assertions that so entertain the architect.

IV

The third attempt to provide a linguistic analysis of architecture is the semantic account rigorously defended by Nelson Goodman. Goodman's thesis is more in line with the teachings of C. S. Peirce. Following Peirce, Goodman takes reference to be a connection between signs and the world. A sign, that is, refers to the world, or some part of it. Like Peirce, Goodman sets about providing a taxonomy of the ways in which signs refer to the world. So

Goodman's account is more classificatory than explanatory and does not share the overblown ambition of the structuralist accounts. Nevertheless it provides an account of meaning and for Goodman, a work of architecture is separated from the quotidian world of mere buildings by demonstrating the feature of reference. Roughly speaking, a building achieves the status of architecture if it can be shown to refer to something other than itself or even to features of itself. However, like the linguistic theories of the structuralists and their surviving post-structuralists, Goodman's account gives no special place to experience.

Moreover, the experience that we have when looking at the Sydney Opera House is not one of understanding references to sailboats. Without my attention being drawn to that aspect of the building, I might well think it beautiful; and think of the great billowing roof-scape as inflated from beneath by the voices of the grand divas and the arias of sopranos, tenors and baritones. Indeed, if we were to look at the concept model that Utzon made for the building in its initial stage, we can see that the roof forms are developed from a consideration of segments of a hemisphere. That might provide me with an appreciation of the building in terms that do not refer to sailboats. The point is that reference is tied up with meaning, and hence understanding, in a much stricter sense than we encounter in aesthetic appreciation. I do not deny there might be some point in seeing the roof-scape as it juts into the harbour as sails. However, this would be a way of filling out the content of the experience, and not as a way of providing the meaning that I must get to via the route of reference supposedly laid down by Utzon in his linguistic efforts to elevate the building into the realm of architecture.

Exemplification and expression fair little better. For one thing, it is not at all clear that these are forms of reference in language. Arne Jacobsen's St Catherine's College, Oxford has a dining hall whose flat roof is supported by beams spanning internal pillars. To that end, the wall is a mere curtain separating outside from in, but supporting nothing above it. Jacobsen shows this by including a glazing strip between the roof and the top of the wall. Now, while attention to this feature is clearly part of what it is to appreciate the building, it is not obvious that this is a case of linguistic reference. My *experience* of the building includes my seeing the strip as revealing the structure of the building. But this is now given as part of what it is to see the building. If we now remember that it is essential to experience that it is present to consciousness, we can be confident that we are locating the meaning of the building within the appropriate mental framework.

AESTHETICS AND ARCHITECTURE

Goodman's conception of architectural interpretation attempted to steer a middle way through absolutism on the one hand – the view that in our grasp of an architectural work, we are constrained by the need to recognize the architect's intention – and radical relativism, the view that any interpretation of the work of architecture is as good as any other. Goodman's third way is reconstructive relativism, where the interpretations of works of architecture are not supposed to aim at truth.

As a matter of fact, this is the position that I would like to adopt in this book. However, I doubt that Goodman is in a position to sustain the view. On Goodman's view, architecture just is building combined with reference. If that is so, then either Goodman must hold that interpretations are secured by reference, in which case they aim at fixed meaning and there is a hard and fast interpretation. Or else, reference is itself insecure, in which case we can never know what anything really means; and that is the position that has been argued for by Derrida and the deconstructionists. (It was an advantage of Goodman's semantic view over the semiologists' view that reference connected signs with bits of the world. Those ties look now as if they are in danger of coming loose.)

However, armed with the distinctions and discriminations made available in the philosophy of mind, we can look again at Wittgenstein's problem concerning interpretation of an ambiguous figure. Interpreting, Wittgenstein reminds us, is putting forward a hypothesis, which can be true or false. Seeing is a state. When I look at my wrist and see the red blotches there, I can interpret them as an allergy to the nickel that is the reverse side of my watch: 'It's an allergic rash'. In making that claim I venture into the world of medical science and I can be right or wrong according to whether the rash is caused by, is a symptom of, the nickel having come into contact with my skin. When I see a face in the clouds I do not make the same kind of claim. 'I see a face', in this instance, makes no claim about the way of the world. Of course, seeing faces in clouds does not call upon our response to the work of anyone; and so it falls short of the kind of judgement we make when we discuss works of architecture. However, if we take this as a case of imaginative seeing, we can add features that carry over into our judgements of works of art and architecture.

When I see the corner of a building as resolving two façades, I am drawing upon my acquaintance with a visual tradition of making buildings. I can both see the problem and I can see how it is that the architect has resolved that problem. Here, however, there is nothing more to the recognition of this feature of the building than my recognition of it from within the history of architecture. It is not as if there is an answer to the question of the corner's resolution that I could call upon independently of my seeing it. Here, recognizing the architect's 'solution' to the collision of façades is more like grasping the point of a clever piece of wit. That is not to say that the enjoyment of wit is radically relativistic. It is merely to say that there is no scientific proof that some comment was deliciously clever. Nevertheless, when we are amused by someone's wit, we attribute intention to him. What we need to strengthen our claim that architectural intention is at the heart of our conception of architecture is a widening of our conception of intention so as to resist the view that the recognition of intention binds us to the view that 'intentionalism' is an absolutist view.

The breadth we need is readily available. Intentions are propositional attitudes, and, as we have seen, these are best understood from the third-person perspective. There are many intentions that I have of which I am unaware. Indeed, if Marx and Freud are to be believed, there are many intentions that I have and that accounts for my actions that are structurally masked out of my consciousness; so that I could not recognize them were I to stare them in the face.[7]

In the next chapter we shall encounter descriptions of architectural experiences that could not, at least as they are described there, be attributed to the architects whose work we are considering. However, I think it sufficient to rely upon the history of architecture, taken broadly, to provide the context within which both the spectator understands the work at which he looks, and the architect forms the intentions that are thereby embodied in the work he builds. The prospect over a landscape that the building fronts onto might have any number of details that make up the spectator's experience. Perhaps a great many of these experiences could not have been foreseen by the architect. Nevertheless, in making a balcony or a panoramic view, the architect creates the conditions within which these particular experiences shall be framed.

V

The introduction of the Situationist International shifted our attention from the work of architecture as a building out there in the world and withdrew it to a middle ground between building and spectator; where the spectator projected his values onto the building. The building, while not conceived as a piece of language, was nevertheless to be conceived as an artefact that contained within it a commitment to a certain sort of life. Thus we were to think of architecture not merely as building there to be used in its inhabitation. Rather, it was to be seen as an outward manifestation of a form of life. That seems to capture something of the importance of architecture for us. It shows us why it is that we must consider architecture to be more than merely functional in either the austere or the aesthetic senses. It is not to be considered austerely functional, as it must be seen as an embodiment of our values. But neither must it be seen as aesthetically functional, since the cultural significance that we now wish to project upon it far outstrips the idea that architecture is merely elegant in its pursuit of everyday purposes.

That is a lesson we must take from the politicization or socialization of architecture. We must now admit that architecture, perhaps more than the other arts, has a part to play in our moral life. What is at issue with the situationists and with other political and social doctrines of architecture is, therefore, the political, social or moral commitments with which the architecture is concomitant. This, however, provides a problem for the view we were putting forward in Chapter 4. Since there we entertained the idea that theory did not aim at truth and the attendant thought was that we should regard theoretical commitments as filters through which to view the work of architecture. The problem now is that these commitments are so much at the heart of the architecture that we cannot so easily disregard them. They have to be taken seriously.

Take, for instance, the Olympic Stadium in Berlin, built for Hitler's 1938 Olympic games. That building contains within its commitments an espousal of National Socialism. Can we merely view the building and think of it 'through the filter of National Socialist commitments'? As a matter of fact, I remember visiting that stadium before its recent refurbishment. And, while the shadow of National Socialism hung heavily over the building, I thought it nevertheless beautiful. I understand why others could not.

In any case, the situationists built nothing of much import. But looking at their writings and viewing some of Asger Jorn's paintings does connect the spectator to the beauty that lies therein, if only he can permit the filter to keep him at a safe distance from the sometimes foolish, sometimes sinister commitments of the artists and architects concerned.

The experience that we have of the works with which we have been considering here, is complex and interweaves the moral and political into the aesthetic. That is a welcome development, since we should feel more comfortable with a view of architectural response in which such complexity abides. How then are we to elucidate such experiences?

VI

When we look at architecture as a public art, in light of the public-art movement, we are able to extend the notion of politics and community that we had introduced when we discussed the Situationist International. The move away from the Romantic view of the artist as a solitary genius, toward the more engaged notion of the artist as a skilled member of a community acting on its behalf in collaboration with it, seems a welcome move; and one that reflects upon the status of architecture as a public art. Moreover, in addressing the nature of Maya Ying Lin's Vietnam War Veterans' Memorial, we were able to see the significance of that piece when compared to a more sculptural monument. It is along the lines of architecture as a public art that we shall proceed in the application of the ideas developed in Chapter 10.

VII

The claim was made earlier that an imaginative experience contains within it descriptions of that which is absent to perception; but which is founded upon the perceived features of some specified part of the environment. We considered the case of depiction in providing an example of what such an experience might be like. In arguing against Goodman we have claimed that his semantic view does not do justice to the experiential character of architectural appreciation. We need, now, to bring these two threads together in such a way that they can pull into focus the appropriate response to architecture.

If imaginative experience contains what is absent from perception, we need to know what, if anything, puts constraints upon or delimits the imagination. Richard Wollheim, in his espousal of the twofold thesis, sets out an example of what can be seen in a painting.

Consider the following experiment: I look at a picture that includes a classical landscape with ruins. And now imagine the following dialogue: 'Can you see the columns?' 'Yes.' 'Can you see the columns as coming from a temple?' 'Yes.' 'Can you see the columns as coming from the temple as having been thrown down?' 'Yes.' 'Can you see them as having been thrown down some hundreds of years ago by barbarians?' 'Yes.' 'Can you see them as having been thrown down some hundreds of years ago by barbarians wearing the skins of wild asses?' (Pause.) 'No.'

At each exchange, what 'Yes' means is that the prompt has made a difference to what has been seen in the scene, just as the 'No' signifies that, for at least *this spectator here and now*, the limits of visibility in this surface have been reached.[8]

What we must take from this example is that the response to the prompt is that to which, for this particular spectator, he is able to assent. In the case of representation this is held to be given in the depiction, provided that the spectator correctly identifies the objects depicted. However, the *question* is whether the spectator can *see* what it is that the prompter puts forward. And so, while the ground for what the spectator sees is out there on the painted surface, the spectator has to have the experience prompted in order to be able to assent. It is not that there is a meaning and the spectator reads it off. Rather, the spectator has an experience which is more or less rich and of which he alone is the arbiter. There is something inviolably subjective about our experience of art in general. However, the above example neatly shows how it is that these subjective experiences can be prompted in us.

In claiming that the imaginative experience is a compound of perception and imagination, we are to understand that we bring that which is absent to perception into the enriched experience. This is a complex thought. It means that the content of imaginative experience is constituted in part by that which is absent; while at the same time resting upon that part of the experience which is present, the perceived work. It is this compound mental state that permits us to think of experiences having a range of both broad and deep contents. Provided, as in Wollheim's hypothetical dialogue, that the spectator is able to see that content, the only constraint upon breadth and depth is the imagination of the spectator himself.

Is there any parallel in the case of architecture? It has been argued that architecture is a visual art; and for this reason it is essential that giving an account of architectural significance must include our visual experience of the work. In looking at paintings we considered the imaginative experience of 'seeing' the representational content of the work while perceiving the worked surface of the canvas. The imagined experience abides with the perceived canvas. In architecture we perceive the building as we look at it from a distance, enter it, put it to use and make our departures. Wherein lies the counterpart with imaginative experience? It is this question to which we now turn.

CHAPTER 12

REPRESENTATION AND EXPRESSION: ARCHITECTURAL ALLUSION AND FRAMES

I

In Chapter 9, we considered Maya Ying Lin's Washington Vietnam Veterans' Memorial; and argued that the experience it afforded was architectural rather than sculptural, calling, as it does, upon architectural responses. We briefly mentioned the sculpture of the three serving soldiers, standing just a few yards away from Ying Lin's beautiful piece of work, which does not elicit any architectural response. But can architectural significance include the representational? And can it include the expressive? If it cannot, then how best must we conceive architectural significance?

The representational arts are those which provide us with descriptions or depictions of the world as they suppose it to be. Visual representations, rather than linguistic representations, provide us with access to the visual properties of the supposed world. We see an object or scene and our visual awareness of that object or scene can contain everything that we can ordinarily see in the world when we put our perceptual apparatus under its usual obligations. We see, for instance, a man on a horse when we look at a portrait of Wellington; or we see the humiliation of man as this particular man is tossed around on a blanket held in the hands of surrounding women in Goya's *Feminine Folly*. The limits of what we can see represented in a picture track the limits of what we can see in our normal observation of the world. (We can see a winged horse flying toward the sun in a representation because, were there to be such things and were they to enter into such events, we could see them with our perceptual apparatus.)

Expression, and its presence in the arts, provides us with a dimension of experience concerned not with how things look, but rather with how things feel to us. The emotions we feel in listening to a piece of music in some way track the emotions we feel in real life. I am supremely grateful that I feel no obligation to construct a theory of the emotions nor yet a theory of expression derived from it. In this chapter I want only to consider the way in which architec-

REPRESENTATION AND EXPRESSION

ture can be said to express mental states; and my strategy shall be to compare it and contrast it with the other expressive arts in order to see how much can be said of architecture's facility for expression.

Our question, then, is this: in what sense can we think of architecture as being an art that derives its aesthetic character by visually representing the world; or by expressing mental properties such as the emotions that we hear in music?

We have already considered the classical attempt to provide a mimetic account of architecture. And we resisted that account on the grounds that architecture, at least as it is to be found in classicism, could not be given a representational treatment as it is implausible to conceive of all classicism in terms of intended representation. Goodman's citing Utzon's Sydney Opera House as denotative, might strike us as a case of intended representation. Taken case by case, we might think, architecture might be representational, just if the architect intends the building to be seen as a representation of this or that. And surely the fibreglass hamburger-stand, shaped and coloured as a giant hamburger, is a case of a building that is representational.

Let us take these two cases side by side. The Sydney Opera House, considered as a representation of sailboats, is poor. That is to say that we could think of a better representation of sailboats. We could think of a sculpture of sailboats that jut out into the harbour; a sculpture that would be more true to the experience of looking at sailboats. Here, what guides our thought is the degree of naturalism that sculpture affords. And if then, by way of criticism, we thought that, as a sculpture, we would want not a mere simulacrum of sailboats but something of the essence of sailing and the thrill of sailing, we might recommend to the sculptor that he make his work less realist with respect to how sailboats look; and more realist with respect to the experience of sailing; or to watching sailboats course through the waters. That is to say that we would ask the sculptor to exploit his medium in bringing out some aspect of sailing. Now, the architect might counter that it is only as a sculptural representation that the Sydney Opera House is poor. As an *architectural* representation it is fine. But we do not have a cogent understanding of what an architectural representation is. And this is brought out if we now turn to the hamburger-stand. For in thinking of the giant hamburger shape with its naturalistic form and colour we find that we have an experience as of looking at a huge hamburger. At the intersection between representation and building, we see the poor soul who vends the sandwiches gazing out at us. We think it an intrusion into the experience of the representation; an intrusion to be masked out as best we can. That is to say that when we look at naturalism as a feature of our supposed architectural representation, we find that the use to which the 'work' is put, the selling of fast foods, mars the very experience the 'work' is supposed to afford. In the case of the opera house, by contrast, we find that the lack of naturalism leaves us no alternative representational feature with which to replace it. Architecture, in the case of the opera house, is simply not up to the task of representing sailboats.

If architecture is not a representational art, then what must we say about these two examples? I think it fair to say that Utzon's building is not a representation; but that there is an allusion to the billowing sails in the roofline of his building. That allusion can feature in the experience we have of the building and can be partially contributive to the aesthetic character that the building displays. However, it does not seem proper to say of someone who does not recognize the allusion, that they have misunderstood or not understood the building; as surely Goodman would have to say. In this sense we could say that architecture admits of allusion, while falling short of fully fledged representational properties.

Of the hamburger-stand, we should think that the building represents a hamburger; but that it does so sculpturally. As a putative work of architecture the representational aspect is a hindrance to our understanding. It gets in the way of our thinking of the building, *as a building*. Indeed, since the only way to impose itself upon us is with its high degree of naturalism, we might say that this is a poor piece of work in that the sculptural aspect of the hybrid work does not engage the imagination in any way that is aesthetic. It provides us with an experience as of a giant hamburger, spoilt only where the architectural aspect intrudes. The experience as of a giant hamburger, however, is an experience that is impeded in its aesthetic development by its requirement to remain wholly naturalistic. That is to say that the attempt at naturalistic representation in architecture fails because it does not have the facility of allusion.

II

In looking at our responses to architecture, when considering the situationists, we were able to introduce the spectator and his conception of moral and political matters into our understanding of architecture. We might now look at allusion along these lines. The

REPRESENTATION AND EXPRESSION

theoretician Penny Florence asked us to consider the gaze of the artwork as it fixes the spectator.[1] In considering architecture we might think of ourselves as the objects of spectatorship, when taking up occupancy of a building. Or again, it might be useful to think of our gaze, when we look at the building, being returned when we admire it from the outside. The building, that is, can be seen as taking up an attitude toward us. This way of conceiving our spectatorship invokes allusion.

What are we to make of expression? 'Architecture is music in space, as it were a frozen music', says Friedrich Wilhelm Joseph von Schelling; and sometime later: 'I call architecture frozen music', says Johann Wolfgang von Goethe. Do buildings, then, express emotions or other states of mind in the same way as symphonies and sonatas? It would not seem that the comparison stands up to scrutiny. Like representation in painting and sculpture, music is more plastic than architecture and therefore more able to deal with a range of emotions. It is difficult to think of the extreme sadness or grief that we hear in Brahms's *German Requiem* as having a counterpart in architecture. Architecture surrounds us and forms an integral part of our daily lives. We cannot escape it. What would be the musical equivalent of that? In 1989, when the Americans' removed General Manuel Noriega from his *de facto* military leadership of Panama, the United States military, in a bizarre emulation of Francis Ford Coppola's scene in *Apocalypse Now*, blasted the papal nuncio day and night with heavy rock music's most expressive and bombastic passages. Poor man. That is torture. (It would only have been surpassed in its horror and would surely have constituted a war crime had they bombarded him with Fifty Cent.)

The art of architecture is quieter than music, so to speak. It does not claim our attention in the way that music is entitled to demand. Being ever present and essentially public, architecture is called upon to abide with us in peaceful harmony. The pleasure it affords, therefore, is less exacting in its calling upon our concentration; and more accommodating in its supporting a 'picture' of how we might live.

The point is that architecture cannot hope to have the same expressive range as music. Is it then a restricted form of expressive art? However, that would mean that, as an art, it was inferior to music. That hardly makes sense. Architecture is an art in that it provides us with accommodation; and in so providing it addresses our appreciation of the lives we live within its embrace. Architecture is not inferior to music. The individual arts are not in that sort of competition. Architecture, however, does have the power to move us, emotionally. We remember Goodman's description of the expressive Gothic cathedral that 'soars and sings'. If, as I have claimed, architecture is not expressive in the same way as music, we might consider revising this description. It is not that the Gothic cathedral expresses an emotion. Rather, it alludes to a certain attitude that we should take up toward the building once we inhabit its spaces. We think of a certain sort of attitude that we are called upon to strike up toward the building once we are in its space.

III

It is with the notion of architectural allusion that we must now grapple. Allusion, as that is to be found in the literary arts, is the means by which an author deliberately makes reference to another work, or to an historical event or to whatever it is that the reader takes up as reference from the work he is considering. However, we have seen that in literature, the workings of language engage our imagination in a different way from that in which it is engaged in the visual arts. In the visual arts, we have an experience that is latched onto the perception of the art object in front of us or surrounding us or that we surround.

If there is to be anything distinctive about allusion in the visual arts, we might therefore expect to locate it in the relation held between perception of the work of architecture and the imaginative experience that is there grounded. Unlike depiction, the imaginative experience is not fastened to the perceived surface. However, like depiction, the perception of the architectural work is the ground for the imaginative experience. Like depiction, there are two features of the experience, each of which must be given its due. In the first place there is the perception of what is there in front of you, the building as it is seen by walking round and through it; by inhabiting it. Then there is the allusive qualities that are brought to mind by the work at which you gaze. These qualities can be brought to bear upon our experience, as when I look at San Carlo alle Quattro Fontane and consider its relation to the classical orders; or when I look at Sydney Opera House and consider the allusion to sailboats; or when I stand beneath a lanterned dome and consider the relation between the temporal and the eternal, using my perception of falling light to give experiential content to my ruminations.

Perhaps, we might think, when Picasso paints his variations on

REPRESENTATION AND EXPRESSION

Velázquez's *Las Meninas*, the maids of honour are depicted in his painting; but Velázquez's painting is alluded to in the later work. In both cases the experience is connected to the perceived paint surface. However, in the case of allusion, the work of the original artist forms something against which to see the variation. Architecture, in this respect, has the same facility of allusion as do the other arts.

IV

Is allusion the sole source of meaning in architecture? We have drawn upon the philosophy of mind to establish the fact that over all the arts it is the imaginative experience we have that locates value. There is much that we experience in our appreciation of architecture; and allusion was introduced so as to show how it is that, even when falling short of fully fledged representation or expression, architecture had the capacity of allusion. That was to explain the intuition some have had that it was possible for architecture to represent and to express; and to replace representation and expression with a notion that would be acceptable. It was not, however, to circumscribe the means by which we come to appreciate architecture.

On Christmas Day 2004, I found myself in a hotel bar with my wife sipping cocktails, overlooking the River Plate in Montevideo. The river had a greyish pink opacity and seemed to lighten as a storm developed and the sky darkened to the colour of slate washed with indigo. Through some moments there seemed to be a light emanating from the river, albeit dimly. The warm rain fell in dark veils like swirling glazes across an immeasurable canvas. The swathes of rain obscured the horizon along stretches of the river; so that for some passages sky and river melded. Flashes of lightning punctuated our lazy drinking; and made us suddenly aware of the room in which we stood. And the grumble of thunder gave cathartic release to the humid tension that had accumulated in the Uruguayan summer. The scene outside reminded me of a painting that the New York painter, Tim Kent, was then working on in his studio; although the colour combination was like nothing I had seen before in nature or in art.

The hotel is an undistinguished piece of modernism. Its bar presents a vast panorama through its floor-to-ceiling glass façade on its second floor. The vista is too wide to be taken within the cone of vision; and so I had the feeling that the vastness of the river itself intruded upon, as well as surrounded, our social space. It was grander than cinematic. Brandy Alexander much improved our mood as did the convivial conversation which sauntered along languidly and pointlessly through the morning and into the afternoon. That was a beautiful day. I wonder if I would have thought it so beautiful to be standing by the side of the river, exposed to the turmoil of the entangled elements. I cannot say. However, I can say with confidence that the beauty of that day was constituted in part by the architecture we inhabited.

Had it not been for the design of that panoramic glazing, on the second floor overlooking the river, the greatest part of the aggregated properties of that experience would not have been available. Some of those properties were to be shared between us as we stood looking out. Others, as with the comparison of the scene with Tim Kent's painting, could be had only by tying up this experience with an acquaintance of the painting.[2] And so, like many aesthetic experiences, possibly all, there was a mixture of shared judgement and solitary pleasure. This, we might feel, is an example of architecture operating *sotto voce*; the quietness of architecture we mentioned earlier. Architecture has the ability to provide us with experiences that do not hold our focus on the building itself, but that organize our experiences as we look out from or away from the building; rather in the way that a frame might enhance a painting. Framing, in fact, is one of the major ways in which architecture contributes to the aesthetic apprehension of everyday life. In describing my Christmas of 2004, I said that it was a beautiful *day*. So here we can see that part of the aesthetic concerns of architects is to do with what the building makes available to us in the pursuit of an aesthetic engagement beyond the work concerned. In this, it has a social value that we find in the other arts; as when my reading a novel or watching a film inspires me to behave in a certain way; or gets me to understand a point of view previously opaque to me. I begin to see the world, and my part in it, as a work of fiction in which I can direct my own character. If the novel makes this available to me; film and painting too, we might easily remember the part that architecture plays in the novel, the film, and painting. Architecture, we might say, is the frame within the frame of film, literature and painting.

If I can come to regard architectural features as framing the activities with which others pursue their lives, then I can come to see those frames as regulatory over my own activities as I press ahead with my ambitions. Lives, constituted by projects of one sort or another, are accommodated in the environment we construct around those projects. 'The creation of architecture', Asger Jorn has told us, 'implies the construction of an environment and the establishment of a way of life'. The dignity of those projects, of our lives, we might think, is made concrete in the architecture within which they are prosecuted. It is a very obvious point, but I shall make it in any case: that the stage set lends value to the plot and to its unravelling before an audience, so architecture lends value in its contribution to the sense of our unfolding lives.

CHAPTER 13

ARCHITECTURE AS A FORM OF LIFE

I

Consider two questions. What is the nature of tradition in architecture; and what part does architecture, as a visual art, play in the lived world? (Perhaps these two questions are really only one). In Part II we looked at the nature of meaning in architecture as that might be imported from our conception of language. We found that model inadequate to our purposes. Architecture is an abstract visual art and, at various points in this book, its significance – the manner in which we apprehend architecture – has been compared and contrasted with that of representational painting. Perhaps, though, considering the nature of tradition and its place in our lives, we might start by looking at architecture in terms of its vernacular. For it is in the everyday world of architecture that we can come to see that art is connected with our way of living.

In the development of aesthetics, philosophers have been concerned with questions about the character of art taken broadly: its ontology, its relation to nature, its connections with the other human disciplines; or with questions concerning the 'pure' arts: for instance, painting, music and poetry. There is one philosopher, Roger Scruton, who has a special concern with architecture and has written extensively about it.[1]

Throughout his work in this area we are reminded that what might otherwise be thought to 'contaminate' architecture (its functionality) is that which makes it human. Scruton's enduring disdain for modernism gets a firm grip in the humdrum realm of building, where art and world are bonded. When we considered architecture as a public art, we put a distance between the pursuit of building and the Romantic idea of the artist as genius. Furthermore, from the spectator's point of view, we might think that the reception of architecture, its appreciation, is a matter for everyone to celebrate. The aesthetic attitude toward things is not to be regarded as some exceptional capacity of the intellect, available only to the trained expert. Rather, it is an integral part of our rationality. 'In contemplating

ARCHITECTURE AS A FORM OF LIFE

[these things] we bring ourselves into a lived relation with the world, and sense our own part in its design and order.'[2]

Architecture, its sense of order, its place in our lives (both practical and aesthetic) is not the province of the 'artist as genius'. Of Quinlan Terry, Scruton writes: 'His achievement is . . . to have constructed buildings which disappear into their background as though they have been there forever. He takes us back to an architecture . . . whose merit lies precisely in the fact that it requires no genius but only education.'[3] In the last chapter we were brought to see that architecture is quieter than music. It makes fewer demands upon us and it is at once more serious – it forms the background against which we lead our lives – and it is less important – it does not require our constant and undivided attention. Scruton takes this point seriously. In our daily existence we do not seek for stunning new effects or for the work that shines above all others. Instead we seek comfort and solace, immersing ourselves in communities that have developed ways of life to provide exactly that. We place ourselves as individuals in the history of the communities to which we belong and to which, through the benefits of belonging, we owe a duty.

> Through aesthetic reflection we endeavour to create a world in which we are at home with others and with ourselves: and home is not a home without the implication of community. Home is not occupied only by us: it is inhabited by the ghosts of our ancestors, and by the premonition of children that are yet to be. Its essence is continuity, and it provides the archetype of every experience of peace.[4]

Architecture, then, is the art which most naturally encapsulates what has been called a 'form of life'. Without the need for genius and with tradition placed at the centre of our understanding (both of what architecture is and of its importance in human affairs) Scruton is in a position to give a critical appraisal of the classical vernacular, defending it against its detractors and regarding its merits when set beside the legacy of modernism. The good manners of the classical pattern book provide guidance for the educated builder, whereas the extravagant intellectualism of the would-be modernist genius is an affront to any who would live in an educated democratic community. Of the classical vernacular in London he says: 'The politeness of the style – the refusal to outrage or to defy – reminds one constantly of the ideal condition of society, in which people seek to co-operate, and in which conversation takes the place of command'.[5]

Scruton seems to place the blame for modern architecture on modernism and sees that as stemming from the same philosophy of social science that gave rise to the centrally planned economy. The problem is that modern architecture is doing very well in late-capitalist liberal democracies; witness the skyline of New York, Chicago or even London; consider the rapidly developing Far Eastern capitals. The nihilism of our age is as virulent and effective in the architecture of modern liberal states (and in the conception of the self which sustains them) as it could ever have hoped to be under socialism. Does Scruton's aesthetic argument, then, turn us back toward a pre-modern world? Not exactly.[6] Scruton stops short of the religious conviction that might have been invoked to recall a greater past. Indeed, it may well be this reticence which makes him cling to classicism. 'The classical temple marks out an inner sanctum in the space of our world, while the Gothic cathedral is the gateway to another space, potentially infinite and outside the sphere of daily life.'[7] This contrast between the classical and the Gothic tends toward a vision of the former as secular or, at any rate, non-theistic. The use of the pagan temple, as the foundation of a view of ourselves in an age which has lost touch with religious sensibility, is what marks out Scruton's case as itself nihilistic. His passion is for a world which is to him irredeemably lost. A true believer, whose ties to the past are unbroken by the torrents of Enlightenment philosophy, might feel no need to establish himself in the artificial sanctity of a classical past.

Modern orthodoxy, however, is secular. Within that orthodoxy, but against the trend, Scruton makes claim for a more civilized visual world. On his view our interest in all that is visual, an interest in the meaning of appearances, is an interest in the world independent of the purposes which are ours. In the last chapter we argued for the place that experience holds in our understanding of the aesthetic in architecture. We developed that view in order to reject the claims of the orthodoxy that has emerged through structuralism and its inversion post-structuralism. Architecture is functional, but inhabiting the built environment and coming to see its significance lies beyond any singular purpose which we might have. 'One must not think that because we now see art as purposeless, we also see it as without value. Peace, love and friendship are purposeless, precisely because they contain their value within themselves. The same is true of art.'[8]

Scruton's work puts aesthetics at the heart of philosophy, at once proclaiming the importance of appearances and establishing the weight that they must be made to bear. In looking at architecture he has focused on the importance of the everyday world in which we are consigned to lead our lives. Architecture, art and design are intimately bound up with what we are. A sense of the self-in-the-world is what is at stake in this enterprise. Visual art and architecture, on such a view, are a part of the visual world which is made to reveal the status of our selves. It is, of course, just such a view that I propose in this book.

Nevertheless, it would be a mistake to remove our purposes entirely from our conception of art and architecture. Rather we should regard designed objects as imaginatively 'picturing' our purposes or alluding to them, and, in so capturing the 'appearance' of our purposes, we see these objects as lending dignity to our lives. The shared uses to which designed objects are put reveal the form of life in which a community persists. It is to the form of life that we allude when we bring imaginative experience to supervene upon our architectural perceptions.

II

Michael Podro, in setting out what he envisaged as the 'critical history of art', distinguishes between two types of question. The first kind he calls archaeological, the second, critical. Answering the first kind involves establishing matters of fact and locating sources, patronage and engaging in other aspects of scholarly activity. The second kind of question 'requires us to see how the products of art sustain purposes and interests which are both *irreducible* to the conditions of their emergence as well as *inextricable* from them'.[9] I believe that any account of the critical history of art will rely upon a view of the imagination and its place in sustaining our conception of art taken broadly; and of the particular arts once they have been delineated. Understanding architecture, as with understanding the other arts, on this view, requires imagination.

The architect builds a world in which we see out the compass of our allotted time. He deals with the particularities of materials, their relative strengths, their fitness for purpose and so on. He has to combine these elements in a way which makes a place worthy to serve the purposes of the community for whom it is built. Philosophical questions arise about the value of a work of architecture and what our appropriate response to such a work might be. As Scruton has said, a community lives beyond the limits of the years God grants to each of its members. In considering such general thoughts we can ask: 'What is architecture and wherein lies its value?' Are there enduring principles of architecture which survive the vicissitudes of fashion or style? We can ask of any principle of any historical period of architecture, if any of them endure or survive the change through which the history of architecture passes. Moreover, if we think of the principles embedded in each and every work of architecture as submitting to some hierarchy, we can ask which principles, at the most general level, persist through the history of architecture? Are there enduring principles of architecture which provide an aesthetic account rich enough to accommodate the local and historical particulars of architecture; where these particulars are to be thought more important than fashion or style? Could these principles be different in kind from those derived from the mere fact of history? Could there be principles derived from the very concepts we use when dealing with architecture which would provide a framework within which to understand the particularities of architectural works? This 'conceptual analysis' need not fall into essentialism or what has fashionably come to be known as 'logocentricism'. We need only ask of our current usage of the term 'architecture' what principles can be derived from *its* use that clear matters up, or that help us to understand better the nature of the beast at which we stare.

III

In Chapter 7 we rehearsed Goodman's account of how architecture at its most general can be conceived. In his essay, 'How Buildings Mean'[10] Goodman gave a range of examples including twelfth-century French Romanesque, eighteenth-century German baroque, and more recent buildings by Utzon, Gaudi and Rietveld. Goodman's analysis of architectural meaning aims to account for all architecture. In so doing, he makes an ahistorical claim for the nature of that understanding and were that claim to take hold of us, we would be constrained in looking at architecture to explain the work under view in terms of its reference. Goodman's argument is an account of what is constitutive of our concept of architecture. For Goodman, it is a building plus reference; it is a building plus meaning. In what follows below, I hope to provide an alternative account of our concept of architecture, but one which competes with Goodman's account at that same general level. Nothing concerning particular styles is established in such an account. If what I say is persuasive, it will prompt us to think that any work of architecture in any style requires the kind of experience of which I speak.

In considering works of architecture – works specifically brought into being to serve our purposes – we do not merely inhabit buildings in order to proceed with the commerce of daily life. We prefer some buildings to others just as we find we have preferences in the other arts, preferring this library by Colin St John Wilson to that by Asplund, for instance; (or vice versa). If the kind of explanation of our preferences in architectural matters tracks the kind of explanation of our preferences in the other arts, then perhaps we have reason to think that, at least at some general level, there is a certain *kind* of experience in which these preferences find their justification. We have argued in Chapter 10 that the kind of experience we need to call upon – in order to account for our appreciation of works of art (including architecture) – is an imaginative experience. Given that imaginative experience is at the heart of our appreciation of the arts in general, what in particular, pertains to architecture as an art?

IV

We have considered the different kinds of imaginative enterprise undertaken when considering our reading of novels and our looking at paintings. Our reactions to pictures are *in some sense* like our reactions to what they depict.

> It is useful to introduce the idea of a picture-object. For instance, ☺ would be a 'picture-face'.
> In some respects I stand towards it as I do towards a human face. I can study its expression, can react to it as to the expression of the human face. A child can talk to picture-men or picture-animals, can treat them as it treats dolls.[11]

Here Wittgenstein builds into the nature of the experience a certain way of behaving on the part of the spectator. Our reaction to picture-objects engages our dispositions to act in the world – it engages our agency, so to speak. It does so just because we are connected to picture-objects in similar sorts of ways in which we are connected to real objects – by sight. The fact that these reactions are grounded in *imaginative* experience provides resistance to the thought – expressed in certain ideological positions – that the importance of works of art resides in their social or political *consequences*.

AESTHETICS AND ARCHITECTURE

Just because these imaginative experiences are connected to the world in ways that track our ordinary experiences of the world, political and social concerns are not precluded from the aesthetic project into which the artist has entered. As it were, social and political projects can enter into the aesthetic realm by being imaginative presentations – by being fictional.

It is just because of this peculiar feature of our apprehension of pictures that painters have been able to develop and exploit the nature of representation in such a way that the depicted space can be seen to include the spectator. There is a claustrophobic inclusion of the spectator in Tim Kent's painting, *Weight of a Feather III – Ascension*. There is also a systematic framing, albeit in this case of absent figures. The spectator finds himself in the architectural space as the sole occupant, reversing the natural role of looking. The depicted space is usually thought of as being looked into. Here the

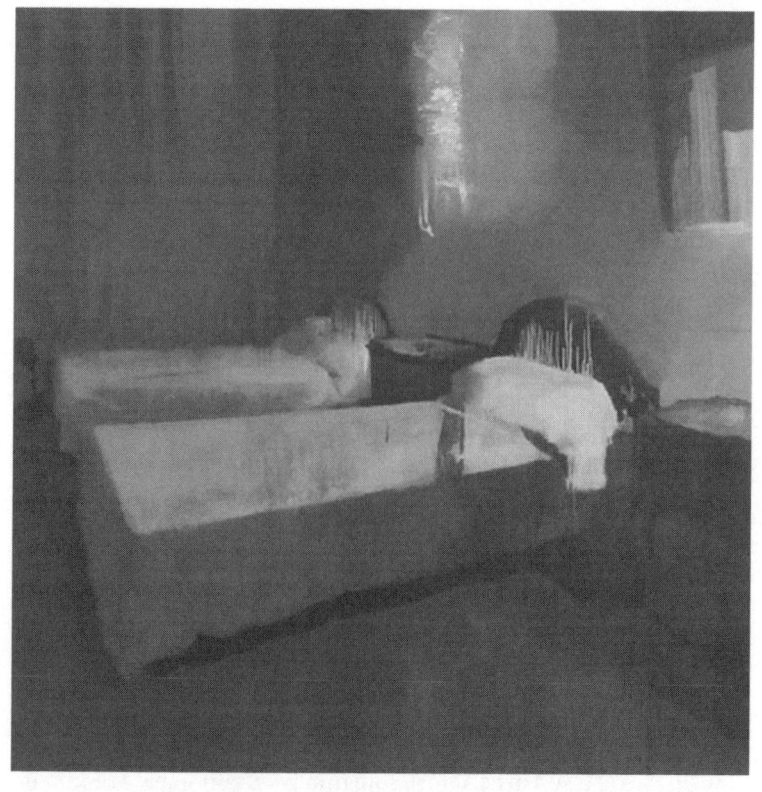

8 Tim Kent: *The Weight of a Feather III – Ascension*

spectator is, to some degree, included in the picture space; whilst that which is usually the object of the spectator's attention, the figure framed in the picture, is absent.

V

Derek Matravers has argued for an affective theory of the emotions as these are suffered in the presence of a work of art. He tells us that reading a novel is fictionally like reading a report.[12] I know the fiction is not true and so I am to imagine that the report belongs to a fictional world in which there are such characters and that these characters are possessed by such and such moral inclinations. Being report-like, the narrative of the novel keeps us at a distance from the action, so to speak. I take him to believe that narrative paintings keep us at a similar distance from the action. Normally, in confrontations with real moral situations, the beliefs that I have with respect to the situation and my place within it, will provide motivation for me to act in a certain way – it will excite my dispositions. In fictions, however, the distance from the moral content provided by the opacity of the work of art prevents us from being so motivated. Compare this with our reactions to documentary reports and documentary photography where we think now of the medium as transparent.

I agree with Matravers that our beliefs about situations and our places within them provide the occasion for action based upon our dispositions and the motivation that these situations provide. I agree with him, further, that when reading fictions, the imaginative project disconnects our dispositions from the motivational force of the imagined moral scene. I do not (and I am not inclined to) rush on stage to save Desdemona from Othello's murderous rage. I agree with him too that looking at a painting is not just the same as being confronted with the depicted scene. However, I disagree with him that our responses to paintings are distanced in the same way as our responses to literary fictions. This matters because I want to claim that in looking at some paintings I become engaged in a way that is similar in some respects to the way I would be engaged in encountering the content of a painting. As Ruby Meager once put it, first asking Wittgenstein's question, then answering it:

Wittgenstein: 'When I see the picture of a galloping horse – do I merely know that this is the kind of movement meant? Is it superstition to think I see the horse galloping in the picture? – And does my visual impression gallop, too?' Answer: who knows, but the gallop can certainly get into my imagination, and, whatever Wittgenstein may say, into sensations in my muscles and my joints, too. That is, if it is a really good picture of a galloping horse.[13]

Here, I think, we can begin to recognize an important feature of the visual arts. The feature is that of perceptual imaginative engagement. While architecture, by and large, has no content – it is, with few exceptions, an abstract art – it is similar to painting in that we take up an imaginative stance toward it. Wittgenstein's example of the child talking to a picture-man, treating the picture-man as she would a doll seems to me to illuminate the character of architecture. When I look at a building, I see in it a certain sort of life – feel that certain sorts of behaviour fit the character of the building. I can feel at home or elevated, can feel its dignity or its meanness. I can sense the history of the people who have occupied it. Here, perhaps, we can borrow from Ruby Meager and say that we do not just look at the building, abstractly assessing its composition as one might a pattern. When I look at a building, or walk around and through it, I feel the life that belongs there. So that the symbolism engages my occupancy. It is not merely a building with added meaning that I read off and thereby understand. In appreciating the building I project a form of life into it. This imagined form of life can more or less accommodate me. Wittgenstein remarks: 'Remember the impression one gets from good architecture, that it expresses a thought. *It makes one want to respond with a gesture.*'[14]

VI

An earlier draft of Chapter 7, on Goodman's semantic view, elicited a written response from the Hungarian-born English poet George Szirtes. In his response Szirtes describes a courtyard in Budapest; and, in so doing, he aims to provide the kind of experiential description which, because of its detail, lies beyond the scope of any general or theoretical description. Of the courtyard he writes:

> It is in a street called Magyar utca, or 'Hungarian Street'. I don't think this fact is of any significance except that it shows that the quarter of the city to which it belongs was probably a foreign quarter – probably Serbian – and that Hungarians there were the

ARCHITECTURE AS A FORM OF LIFE

exception. I also know that the area, and that street in particular, was, up to the end of the second world war full of bordellos... The doorways, as in most Budapest tenements are important as transitions between public (street) and private (yard). Often a cool breeze creeps out of such doorways as a relief from the stifling summer heat outside. They also keep out the noise. Yard noises are private noises: rattlings of pans, conversations, radios, swimming in silence. There is something churchlike about a courtyard – it is a sanctuary – its sanctuarial aspect is probably intentional. As some courtyards have wells or fountains their sanctuarial practical purpose is clear...

Once it must have been rich: the floor is paved with wooden cobblestones, the glass of the windows is thin and buckled. The building has not been cleaned for a long time so the surfaces have grimed to an even warm greyness. The space is small but beautifully proportioned – it seems as necessary as the sound box of a violin or cello; it has to be that size and shape to produce the best sound. Pigeons roost on the ledges and flap across sometimes and you see their reflections flicker and fragment in the windows. Sometimes one becomes aware of people coming down the stairs, which are hidden in the doorway, or one hears one of those courtyard domestic noises I have already mentioned. One knows the place is inhabited by a variety of people, that it has been inhabited before – that people have hidden, died, argued, made love and been born here, and that this is a continuum, something that will go on happening; more, that in this continuum there resides something specific and symbolic of a particular people. I also know, of course – that my personal history is intimately interwoven with this symbolism.[15]

Compare this description of Szirtes' experience of the Budapest courtyard with this of a refurbished college building in St Andrews by John Haldane:

As part of a university-wide policy of continuous improvement it was decided that the building needed extensive refurbishment and that process has been started. Curious to see what might lie in store for us I went to look at another department whose historical building had recently had the same treatment. I am not quite sure what I expected but it was not what I found. The interior had been re-fashioned in what might be termed 'accountancy service style'. You enter a building of muted colours and grey carpets and find a foyer with chairs and plants. It is certainly airy and pleasant but what it entirely fails to offer is any sense of either the history of the building or of its being a place of higher learning. It is devoid of any sense or purpose other than general utility. There are no portraits of former professors or any other historical or academic points of reference.

Overall this constitutes a largely unwitting retreat from the aspiration to do something culturally or ideologically significant with one's environment. Instead there is formal design and decoration achieving a pleasing but unassertive form. This explains the anonymous quality, for it could be any kind of upgraded office. The design is shaken free from any of the particular resonances associated with the nature of the subject practised there, the history of the building itself and the ancient traditions of the University. I leave it as an exercise for the reader to consider how post-ideological pragmatism expresses itself in other aspects of university life.[16]

These descriptions reveal, I believe, a great deal about the nature of architectural experience, given that our appreciation of architecture connects us to a view of life in which it invites us to participate. We see the building and its details as continuous with our projects and our purposes, giving them visual form, so to speak. We see the detail as belonging to our lives in the fashion of lives that have passed before; and so we see our lives projected not only into the building but into its past and its future. Our conception of ourselves as persons may itself be an imaginative project. If it is so, as some have thought, then our conception of ourselves is itself bound up with aspects of a world designed to embrace the projects of that imagined life. Thus I can come to see the purposes of my life accommodated in the significance of the buildings which I inhabit. The accommodation of those purposes is symbolically embedded in the designed world.

I have said nothing of styles of architecture and this is because any such general theory leaves out such detail. In quoting from Szirtes' letter, I wanted to show what one kind of engaged experience of architecture would be like.

The contrast between the 'accountancy service style' of which Haldane has written and the 'purposive humanism' of which I write, where we are given an architecture that characterizes our purposes in its appearances, might be thought to bring into focus the architectural dimension of the new political divide. I mean by this that if the old divisions between left and right in politics are no longer so clearly drawn, we can instead split political thought clearly between liberalism and the new communitarianism. Modern architecture seems to me to divide between similar allegiances. On the one hand there is architecture that engages the communities that live within its embrace; which binds its inhabitants together, so to speak. On the other hand there are buildings whose formal arrangements are so neutralized that they lack any sense of symbolism and so lack meaning as that can be found in architecture. These buildings precisely fail to deliver us any conception of what they are or of who we are.

Let us conclude by considering a verse from 'The Courtyards' by George Szirtes and the experience to which it alludes:

> the small lift shuts and forces itself up
> a narrow throated shaft with groans of chains
> and pulleys, and the whole building complains;
> but as you rise through slices of pale light
> the brown intensifies to cream, and white,
> a trancelike ring of silence at the top.[17]

Compare that sense of the self in the lift of Szirtes' poem as it groans under our weight, with the lift in the modern office building, say Canary Wharf. That modern lift is de-humanized, like the digitally manufactured 'auto-attendant' of the voice-mail at many corporate headquarters; or the telephonic digitally manufactured 'Vivaldi: *Four Seasons*' that occupies the line between the operator's interception of your call and the recipient's answer. The experience of travelling in that lift does not engage me or mark out any opacity in my purposes. It does not present the building as a field for my activities – as an appearance of a world in which I come to adopt a way of life. It is merely utilitarian; second only in efficiency to the beaming-up machine of the starship *Enterprise*. That contrast, between the lift in the Budapest courtyard and the lift in Canary Wharf, brings me to what I should like to offer as an enduring principle of architecture. It is perhaps best captured by Wittgenstein: 'Architecture immortalizes and glorifies something. Hence there can be no architecture where there is nothing to glorify'.[18] What is glorified, I believe, is a vision of a way of life; it is our conception of ourselves.

In giving voice to this principle I hope to have shown that it is possible to have general principles that lie outside – or at least at the edges – of history. I hope to have shown that these overarching prin-

AESTHETICS AND ARCHITECTURE

9 Sarah Wigglesworth and Jeremy Till: House

10 Sarah Wigglesworth and Jeremy Till: House

ciples provide a framework within which the detail of history and of human experience and purpose is played out. If plausible, it provides reason to think of the philosophy of architecture and the interpretative history of architecture as connected within a hierarchy of thought about human beings and their lives.

Let us conclude this chapter with an example of a work of architecture which I take to be as important as any in the contemporary world. Its importance lies in the fact that it establishes an aesthetic by instantiating a moral view. The building is the house designed and owned by Jeremy Till and his partner Sarah Wigglesworth. It is an energy-efficient, sustainable building. But what is remarkable about the building is that its sustainability and its energy efficiency are not merely the kind of additional features that are unsightly and merely functional clutter. The house, built of bails of straw and sand bags, among other things, takes the political and moral strand of energy conservation and makes a work of architecture in which we find aesthetic pleasure. It is in the fact that the house is built with authority and responsibility that we engage with it at an aesthetic level. Its beauty resides in the political and moral objectives that it rightly pursues. And so, in this one building we can see how it is that practical reason and aesthetic judgement can interweave with each other to the benefit of all.

CHAPTER 14

ARCHITECTURAL THINKING

I

The passage through this book has, I hope, drawn together two strands of thought. The first is that architecture is to be described as a visual art; and that in appreciating architecture we have to attend to the appearance of its individual works. The second strand of thought is that the significance that architecture has, involves our seeing it under imaginative descriptions. The experience of architecture is what is important to us. The protracted discussion of mind in Chapters 10 and 11 provided us with materials out of which we were able to fashion a view of experience as rich and complex, admitting content that might otherwise be thought of as beyond the realm of the visual. Nevertheless it is important to note that in our discussion of our appreciation of architecture we are confined to the experiences through which that appreciation is to be enjoyed.

In this last chapter, I want now to consider a number of cases that look as if they belong outwith the confines of architecture. 'Paper architecture' is the name given in the schools to work prepared for competitions and for exhibitions that is not intended to be built. As such, examples of work from within this domain are sometimes merely image-based. Another example of the kind of work that is pursued in the schools is the architect's 'concept model'. These are (in general) small models that the architect considers as an early distillation of the scheme with which he is involved.

We have seen that the constitution of architectural response resides in the experiences to which it gives rise. In the primary instance, as we might expect, the experience is had by looking at, either from the outside or from the inside, a building that we are reviewing. The point of working out the intrinsic nature of architecture, however, was to delineate the architectural experience from other kinds of experience both within and beyond the arts. With paper architecture, if we are able to locate the experience as architectural, whether or not the object of perception is a building, the experience is sufficient to provide the work with the status of a work of architecture.

The architect's concept model is a slightly more straightforward case in point. The model, to all intents and purposes is indistinguishable on first sight from a sculpture or a sculptural maquette. However, it is the status of the model that we are concerned with. Presumably, the concept model is a means of the architect thinking of the scheme in its germination. Our interest is, therefore, in the relation of this model to the finished building. We do not respond to the model as a sculpture or as a sculptural maquette, since we know that its place in the development of a work of architecture is what secures its significance for the architect. It is this recognition that constrains our understanding.

I think that this has relevance to our attitudes to the various arts in general and adds further weight to the view that we are to understand particular works in accordance with the intentions of the architect. My understanding of paper architecture, therefore, is circumscribed by the thought that what I am looking at has its place in a world in which such drawings, collages, models, computer-generated imagery and so on, derive their value from the notion of a building that itself belongs to architecture.

If this is at all plausible, I think that we can accommodate as wide a range of architectural works as the postmodernists and post-structuralists would want. However, we are in a better place to account for the centrality of architecture as building. Provided that we understand architecture as being centrally located in the realm of the built environment, then we can be as broad in our interpretations of what we count as architectural in our dealings with such works of art. This book has attempted to give a very broad account of architecture, without favouring any particular style. It aims, like the competitors we have considered, to give a comprehensive account of architecture. In pursuing this goal, we have concentrated on the reception of architecture; upon how it is that we appreciate its works.

Architecture is important. I hope to have given some reasons for thinking so; and I hope that I have provided a place within the aesthetic domain that can account for its value.

NOTES

Introduction
1. Immanuel Kant, *Critique of Judgement* (trans. Werner S. Pluhar; Indianapolis: Hackett, 1987), pp. 191–92.
2. See also Roger Scruton, *The Classical Vernacular: Architectural Principles in an Age of Nihilism* (Manchester: Carcanet Press, 1994), p. 106. Scruton, there, tells us that, 'when Moses ascended Mount Sinai to speak to his God, he received not only the laws of his people, but also the plan for a temple'.
3. The terminology is introduced in Edward Winters, 'Architecture', in Berys Gaut and Dominic McIver Lopes (eds), *The Routledge Companion to Aesthetics* (London: Routledge, 2nd edn, 2005), pp. 655–67. However, the distinction, quite probably, has been around a good deal longer than this. Functionalists often slither between the two positions.

Chapter 1
1. Vitruvius, *The Ten Books of Architecture* (trans. M. Morgan; New York: Dover, 1960).
2. Alberti, *Ten Books on Architecture* (trans. J. Leoni; London: Tiranti, 1955); William Chambers, *A Treatise on Civil Architecture* (London, 1757); Demitri Porphyrios, 'Classicism is not a Style', in *Architectural Design* 5/6 (1982), pp. 50–57.
3. Richard Wollheim argues, successfully I believe, that our appreciation of representational paintings requires a twofold experience consisting of two aspects, the configurational (the surface) and the recognitional (the depicted content). Abstract (non-representational) painting is ruled out because it does not furnish the experience with a recognitional aspect. *Trompe l'oeil* is ruled out because it does not (deliberately does not) furnish the experience with a configurational aspect. See his, *Painting As An Art* (London: Thames and Hudson, 1987), p. 62.
4. Ludwig Wittegenstein, *Philosophical Grammar* (ed. Rush Rhees; trans. Anthony Kenny; Oxford: Basil Blackwell, 1974), Part I, no. 118, p. 167.
5. Ibid., Part I, no. 118, p. 168.
6. See John Summerson, *The Classical Language of Architecture* (Cambridge: MIT, 1987).

Chapter 2
1. Kant, *Critique of Judgement*, p. 77.
2. Roger Scruton, 'Kant's Prayer', in *Be Attitudes, Poems and Libretti* (n.p.: The Garsdon Press, 1997).

3 Clement Greenberg, 'Modernist Painting' reprinted in Alex Neill and Aaron Ridley (eds), *The Philosophy of Art: Readings Ancient and Modern* (New York: McGraw-Hill, 1995), pp. 111–17.
4 An intriguing and interesting collection of essays on surrealism and architecture looks afresh at that particular strain of modernism. See Thomas Mical (ed.), *Surrealism and Architecture* (London: Routledge, 2005).
5 Alain de Botton, *The Architecture of Happiness* (London: Hamish Hamilton, 2006), pp. 56–57.

Chapter 3
1 Kant, *Critique of Judgement*, p. 76.
2 Ibid., p.191.
3 Viollet-le-Duc, *Discourses on Architecture* (trans. B. Bucknell; London: Allen and Unwin, 1959), p. 448. For an excellent and detailed account of the relation between functionalism and nineteenth-century organicism, see Caroline van Eck, *Organicism in Nineteenth Century Architecture: An Enquiry into its Theoretical and Philosophical Background* (Amsterdam: Architectura & Natura Press, 1994).
4 Adrian Forty, *Words and Buildings: A Vocabulary of Modern Architecture* (London: Thames and Hudson, 2000), pp. 174–95.
5 Usually attributed to the American modernist, Louis Sullivan.
6 Roger Scruton, *The Aesthetics of Architecture* (London: Methuen, 1979), p. 40.
7 W. K. C. Guthrie, *The Greek Philosophers: From Thales to Aristotle* (London: Methuen, 1967), pp. 126–27.
8 For the most coherent exposition of this view see Terry Eagleton, *The Ideology of the Aesthetic* (Oxford: Basil Blackwell, 1990).
9 Kenneth Frampton, *Modern Architecture: A Critical History* (London: Thames and Hudson, 1985), p. 269.
10 Ibid., p. 129.
11 De Botton, *The Architecture of Happiness*, pp. 44–54.

Chapter 4
1 That is not to say that the philosopher might not have something to say about these matters. Roger Scruton argues cogently for classicism as the best way of building in the western tradition. However, his argument is a critical argument, albeit informed by his philosophical expertise. See Scruton, *The Classical Vernacular*. My point is that there are other methods of building that result in works of architecture. To deny this would be either stubborn or perverted or worse: foolish.

Chapter 5
1 Ferdinand de Saussure, *Course in General Linguistics* (trans. Roy Harris; London: Duckworth, 1983).
2 Ibid., pp. 15–16.
3 Much work in the 'New Art History' derives from theoretical positions to be found in Roland Barthes, *The Elements of Semiology* (trans. Annette Lavers and Colin Smith; London: Cape, 1967) and from within that

NOTES

tradition which stretches back at least until Saussure's *Course in General Linguistics*. In *Elements* (p. 11) Barthes tells us that 'We must now face the possibility of inverting Saussure's declaration: linguistics is not a part of the general science of signs, even a privileged part, it is semiology which is part of linguistics: to be precise, it is that part covering the *great signifying unities* of discourse. By this inversion we may expect to bring to light the unity of the research at present being done in anthropology, sociology, psycho-analysis and stylistics round the concept of signification.'

4   Most translators, commentators and theoreticians use 'signifier' and 'signified' as the translation, respectively, of '*signifiant*' and '*signifié*'. In his translation of Saussure's *Course in General Linguistics*, Roy Harris prefers 'signal' and 'signification' respectively. For the sake of convenience, I adhere to the more broadly accepted translation.
5   Saussure, *Course in General Linguistics*, p. 66. See also, ch. 1, section 1, pp. 65–67.
6   Saussure, *Course in General Linguistics*, p. 121.
7   Ibid., p. 122.
8   Ibid., p. 122.
9   See Stuart Sim, 'Structuralism and Post-structuralism', in Oswald Hanfling (ed.), *Philosophical Aesthetics: An Introduction*, (Oxford: Basil Blackwell, 1992), pp. 405–39.
10 Claude Lévi-Strauss, *The Raw and the Cooked* (trans. J. and D. Weightman; London: Jonathan Cape, 1969), p. 147. Quoted in Sim, 'Structuralism and Post-structuralism', p. 415.
11 Roland Barthes, 'Semiology and the Urban', in Neil Leach (ed.), *Rethinking Architecture: A Reader in Cultural Theory* (London: Routledge, 1997), pp. 166–72.
12 Quoted in Frampton, *Modern Architecture*, p. 271.
13 Norman Bryson, 'Semiology and Visual Interpretation', in Norman Bryson, Michael Ann Holly and Keith Moxey (eds), *Visual Theory* (Oxford: Polity Press, 1991), pp. 61–73 (61).
14 Ibid., pp. 64–65.
15 The study of visual culture or visual theory is a direct descendant of structuralism and semiology; and Bryson is a pivotal figure in its emergence and its imperial governance in the world of art history. See Margaret Dikovitskaya, *Visual Culture: The Study of the Visual after the Cultural Turn* (Cambridge: MIT, 2005).
16 Bryson directs us to Ludwig Wittgenstein, *The Philosophical Investigations* (trans. G. E. M. Anscombe; Oxford: Basil Blackwell, 1963), paragraphs 168–90; and 156–71.
17 Wittgenstein, *Philosophical Investigations*, paragraph 43.
18 Ludwig Wittgenstein, *The Blue and Brown Books: Preliminary Studies for the 'Philosophical Investigations'* (Oxford: Basil Blackwell, 2nd edn, 1969), pp. 4–5.
19 Bryson, 'Semiology and Visual Interpretation', p. 66.
20 Ibid., p. 65.
21 Melvyn A. Goodale and G. Keith Humphrey, 'Separate Visual Systems for Action and Perception', in E. Bruce Goldstein (ed.), *Blackwell Handbook*

NOTES

of Sensation and Perception (Oxford: Basil Blackwell, 2001), pp. 311–43 (312–13).

Chapter 6

1. Roland Barthes, 'The Death of the Author', in *Image-Music-Text* (trans. Stephen Heath; London: Harper-Collins, 1977); Roland Barthes, *S/Z* (trans. Richard Miller; New York: Hill & Wang, 1974), pp. 142–48.
2. Barthes, *Elements*.
3. Jacques Derrida, *Of Grammatology* (trans. G. C. Spivak; Baltimore: Johns Hopkins University Press, 1976). Derrida collaborated on work with postmodern architects Bernard Tschumi and Peter Eisenmann.
4. Forty, *Words and Buildings*, p. 173.
5. Jean-Michel Rabaté, 'Introduction 2003: Are You History?', in John Sturrock, *Structuralism* (Oxford: Basil Blackwell, 2nd edn, 2003), pp. 1–16 (1–2).
6. http://www.archidose.org/Feb99/020199.htm
7. Umberto Eco, 'Function and Sign: The Semiotics of Architecture', in Leach (ed.), *Rethinking Architecture*, pp. 182–202 (184). Eco uses the term 'semiotics'. However, semiotics has a different origin than does semiology. Properly speaking, Eco's work belongs to semiology and not to semiotics. Often the two terms are used interchangeably. Semiotics, however, is a good deal older than semiology. It is also more closely connected to logic than to linguistics, though it is true that there are common areas of interest. Nevertheless, an important difference is that semiotics attempts to chart the ways in which various types of sign are connected with the world; and it does this through individual cases (at the micro level). Semiology, by contrast, is concerned with word–world relations only at the overall (macro) level.
8. Jacques Derrida, 'Why Eisenmann Writes Such Good Books' reprinted in Leach (ed.), *Rethinking Architecture*, pp. 336–47 (338).

Chapter 7

1. Nelson Goodman, *The Languages of Art* (Indianapolis: Bobbs-Merrill, 1968).
2. Nelson Goodman, 'How Buildings Mean', in Nelson Goodman and Catherine Z. Elgin (eds), *Reconceptions in Philosophy and Other Arts and Sciences* (London: Routledge, 1988), pp. 31–48.
3. That notion is given a full treatment in *The Languages of Art*, ch. II, esp. pp. 52–56.
4. Goodman, 'How Buildings Mean', p. 44.
5. Nelson Goodman, 'Variations on Variation – or Picasso back to Bach', in Goodman and Elgin (eds), *Reconceptions in Philosophy*, pp. 66–82 (82).
6. Goodman, 'How Buildings Mean', p. 44.
7. Wittgenstein, *Philosophical Investigations*, p. 212^e.

Chapter 8

1. Roger Scruton, 'Continental Philosophy from Fichte to Sartre', in

NOTES

Anthony Kenny (ed.), *The Oxford Illustrated History of Western Philosophy* (Oxford University Press, 1994), p. 121.
2 Kierkegaard published *Repetition: An Essay in Experimental Psychology*, on the same day as he published *Fear and Trembling: A Dialectical Lyric*. The subtitles attest to the two methods of pursuing his project. Sartre's great work, *Being and Nothingness*, and his *Existentialism and Humanism* are both works of philosophy. However, his trilogy, *The Roads to Freedom* and his novel, *Nausea*, extend and give voice to the existentialist perspective upon life.
3 Kari Jormakka, 'The Most Architectural Thing', in Mical (ed.), *Surrealism and Architecture*, pp. 290–317 (304).
4 Peter Marshall, *Demanding the Impossible* (London: Fontana, 1992), p. 552.
5 Asger Jorn, 'Architecture for Life', *Potlatch* 15 (22 December 1954).
6 David Greene taught at Nottinghamshire Polytechnic Fine Art Department with Victor Burgin in the early 1970s – at a time during which that institution was a leader in the development of conceptual art in Britain.

Chapter 9

1 Kant, *Critique of Judgement*, p. 69.
2 Ibid., p. 191.
3 Ibid., p. 175.
4 Ibid.
5 Ludwig Wittgenstein, *Culture and Value* (ed. G. H. von Wright; trans. Peter Winch; Oxford: Basil Blackwell, 1980), p. 46^e.
6 Ibid., p. 45^e.
7 I am grateful to Simon Sadler for his helpful advice upon matters of fact concerning the two monuments in Washington.

Chapter 10

1 Strictly speaking, propositions are unasserted thoughts; although they share the same grammar as assertions. The embedded thought 'It is raining' in 'If it is raining I shall work at home today' is unasserted. When it is embedded in this sentence, the proposition does not commit the speaker to a belief in the state of the weather. And yet 'It is raining' has the same meaning when stated simply as an assertion as when it is embedded in the compound sentence. Such niceties need not detain us here.
2 'Phenomenology', while being the name of a philosophical doctrine, is used here, and in the analytical tradition, to mean that there is a way things seem to a person. Capturing the phenomenology of an experience is, roughly, giving a descriptive account of how things *appear* to someone. I have never had a migraine attack. However, when sufferers provide an account of the phenomenology of such attacks, we get a picture of the sensations that flood in and around and are disruptive to the sufferer's normal perceptual states; and that thereby incapacitate him. Such accounts do not make reference to how things are out there in the world, but rather describe or capture the way things seem to a sufferer.

NOTES

3   For readers not accustomed to this terminology, 'intentionality' is a technical term. It is the 'aboutness' or 'directedness' of a thought, a linguistic structure or a representation. If I hope for a letter from my friend, then my hope takes an object, in this case my friend's letter, whether or not such a thing exists. If it exists, then the actual letter is the material as well as the intentional object of my hope. If it does not exist 'the virtual letter' is the intentional object of my hope. And in this case, there is no material object of my hope.

4   Colin McGinn considers two taxonomies concerning complex mental states such as 'seeing that it is sunny'. He offers that it is a compound comprising two mental states, made up of a sensation and a propositional attitude in combination; or that it is a single mental state which exemplifies two features. In opting for the compound of two mental states, I am persuaded by the survival of the propositional attitude in cases where a belief is based in perception. That is to say that I presume that the component propositional attitude has the same identity across its participation in the perception and its endurance as a simple belief. On this point in particular and on this section of the chapter in general, I have been strongly influenced by McGinn's perspicuous writings. For those unused to reading in the philosophy of mind, I recommend his *The Character of Mind* (Oxford University Press, 1982). See especially ch. 1. For further detailed discussion of these matters, see his, *The Subjective View* (Oxford: Clarendon Press, 1983); and his, *Mental Content* (Oxford: Basil Blackwell, 1989).

5   Aristotle, *De Anima* (trans. Hugh Lawson-Tancred; London: Penguin, 1986), p. 198.

6   Ludwig Wittgenstein, *Zettel*, (ed. G. E. M. Anscombe and G. H. von Wright; trans. G. E. M. Anscombe; Oxford: Basil Blackwell, 2nd edn, 1967), section 621.

7   This is slightly awkward. Dreams are cases of phenomenological presence to consciousness on my view. That is to say that there is an essential awareness that accompanies the phenomenology. And it is this awareness that I want to call consciousness. So, on my view, we are conscious when we dream.

8   Brian O'Shaughnessy, *Consciousness and the World* (Oxford University Press, 2000), p. 347.

9   Ludwig Wittgenstein, *Remarks on the Philosophy of Psychology*, vol. II (ed. G. H. von Wright and H. Nyman; trans. C. G. Luckhardt and M. A. E. Aue; Oxford: Basil Blackwell, 1980), number 111. Quoted in Malcolm Budd, *Wittgenstein's Philosophy of Psychology* (London: Routledge, 1989), p. 108. Malcolm Budd's book provides an excellent expository account of Wittgenstein's complex and often convoluted thought on these aspects of mind.

10 Wittgenstein, *Remarks on the Philosophy of Psychology*, vol. II, number 131. This is also quoted in Budd, *Wittgenstein's Philosophy of Psychology*, p. 109.

11 Wittgenstein, *Philosophical Investigations*, p. 195^{e}.

NOTES

Chapter 11

1. Saussure, *Course in General Linguistics*, p. 67.
2. John Sturrock, *Structuralism* (Oxford: Basil Blackwell, 2003), p. 36. The embedded quote is to be found at Saussure, *Course in General Linguistics*, p. 68.
3. Wittgenstein, *The Blue and Brown Books*, pp. 1–19. For Hilary Putnam's argument that 'meanings are not in the head', see his 'Brains in a Vat', in *Reason, Truth and History* (New York: Cambridge University Press, 1981), pp. 1–21.
4. Saussure, *Course in General Linguistics*, p. 122.
5. To be sure, we do attend to the experience of language when we read novels or poetry. However, the literary use of language is secondary to the way in which language has a primary function in our lives. Perhaps it is because literary theory is concerned with literature that language has come to seem as if it might provide us with an account of all the arts. However, it is because literature is a special case of language that we might think that it stands in need of an explanation from beyond the philosophy of language. It is because language can be used to represent the world that literature can use language to misrepresent the world; and, thereby, express emotions – rather than represent emotions. It is the primary use of language to represent the world that we must consider if language is to be a model with which to consider the arts.
6. Bryson, 'Semiology and Visual Interpretation', p. 65.
7. For a more detailed version of the nature of intention in the arts see, Edward Winters, 'Aesthetic Appreciation', *The Journal of Aesthetic Education* 32 (July 1998), pp. 1–10.
8. Richard Wollheim, 'On Pictorial Representation', in Rob van Gerwen (ed.), *Richard Wollheim on the Art of Painting: Art as Representation and Expression* (Cambridge University Press, 2001), pp. 13–27 (23–24).

Chapter 12

1. Penny Florence was a participant in a research seminar at West Dean College in July 2004. The seminar brought together artists, philosophers and art historians. I do not know of any writings on this matter, but the idea is, I think, highly pertinent to architectural thinking.
2. Note that while I alone underwent this aspect of the experience, it is not thereby private in the sense that it could only be undergone by me. Others, were they acquainted with the painting, could have been persuaded into the comparison; could have taken up the allusion.

Chapter 13

1. Scruton, *The Aesthetics of Architecture*, and more recently *The Classical Vernacular*.
2. Scruton, *The Classical Vernacular*, p. xvii.
3. Ibid., p. 70.
4. Ibid., p. 16.
5. Ibid., pp. 38–39.
6. See his *Modern Philosophy* (London: Sinclair-Stevenson, 1994). In

NOTES

various passages in this melancholy book, Scruton observes the consolation of religion and demonstrates its power to create a human world of value. All of these musings, however, are accompanied by a view that secures the moral value without recourse to religion. I can find nowhere in the book at which he commits himself to any religious view.
7   Scruton, *The Classical Vernacular*, p. 109.
8   Ibid., p. 151.
9   Michael Podro, *The Critical Historians of Art* (London: Yale University Press, 1982), p. xviii.
10 Goodman, 'How Buildings Mean'.
11 Wittgenstein, *Philosophical Investigations*, Part II, xi, p. 194^e.
12 Derek Matravers, *Art and Emotion* (Oxford: Clarendon Press, 1998), ch. 4.
13 Ruby Meager, 'Seeing Paintings', *Proceedings of the Aristotelian Society*, Supplementary vol. 40 (1966), pp. 63–84 (66).
14 Wittgenstein, *Culture and Value*, p. 22^e.
15 This quotation is from private correspondence.
16 John Haldane, 'Higher Education After Ideology: Whose Crisis? What Knowledge?' in R. Barnett and A. Griffin (eds), *The End of Knowledge in Higher Education* (London: Cassell, 1997), pp. 53–66 (59–60).
17 George Szirtes, 'The Courtyards' from *The Photographer in Winter* (reprinted in George Szirtes, *Selected Poems 1976–1996*; Oxford University Press, 1996), pp. 44–47.
18 Wittgenstein, *Culture and Value*, p. 9^e.

BIBLIOGRAPHY

Alberti, *Ten Books on Architecture* (trans. J. Leoni; London: Tiranti, 1955).
Aristotle, *De Anima* (trans. Hugh Lawson-Tancred; London: Penguin, 1986).
Barthes, Roland, *The Elements of Semiology* (trans. Annette Lavers and Colin Smith; London: Cape, 1967).
——*S/Z* (trans. Richard Miller; New York: Hill & Wang, 1974).
——'The Death of the Author', in *Image-Music-Text* (trans. Stephen Heath; London, Harper-Collins, 1977), pp. 142–48.
——'Semiology and the Urban', in Neil Leach (ed.), *Rethinking Architecture: A Reader in Cultural Theory* (London: Routledge, 1997), pp. 166–72.
de Botton, Alain, *The Architecture of Happiness* (London: Hamish Hamilton, 2006).
Bryson, Norman, 'Semiology and Visual Interpretation', in Norman Bryson, Michael Ann Holly and Keith Moxey (eds), *Visual Theory* (Oxford: Polity Press, 1991), pp. 61–73.
Budd, Malcolm, *Wittgenstein's Philosophy of Psychology* (London: Routledge, 1989).
Chambers, William, *A Treatise on Civil Architecture* (London, 1757).
Derrida, Jacques, *Of Grammatology* (trans. G. C. Spivak; Baltimore: Johns Hopkins University Press, 1976).
——'Why Eisenmann Writes Such Good Books', in Neil Leach (ed.), *Rethinking Architecture: A Reader in Cultural Theory* (London: Routledge, 1997), pp. 336–47.
Dikovitkaya, Margaret, *Visual Culture: The Study of the Visual after the Cultural Turn* (Cambridge: MIT, 2005).
Eagleton, Terry, *The Ideology of the Aesthetic* (Oxford: Basil Blackwell, 1990).
van Eck, Caroline, *Organicism in Nineteenth Century Architecture: An Enquiry into its Theoretical and Philosophical Background* (Amsterdam: Architectura & Natura Press, 1994).
Eco, Umberto, 'Function and Sign: The Semiotics of Architecture', in Neil Leach (ed.), *Rethinking Architecture: A Reader in Cultural Theory* (London: Routledge, 1997), pp. 182–202.
Forty, Adrian, *Words and Buildings: A Vocabulary of Modern Architecture* (London: Thames and Hudson, 2000).
Frampton, Kenneth, *Modern Architecture: A Critical History* (London: Thames and Hudson, 1985).
Goodale, Melvyn A. and G. Keith Humphrey, 'Separate Visual Systems for Action and Perception', in E. Bruce Goldstein (ed.), *Blackwell Handbook of Sensation and Perception* (Oxford: Basil Blackwell, 2001), pp. 311–43.
Goodman, Nelson, *The Languages of Art* (Indianapolis: Bobbs-Merrill, 1968).

BIBLIOGRAPHY

―― 'How Buildings Mean', in Nelson Goodman and Catherine Z. Elgin (eds), *Reconceptions in Philosophy and Other Arts and Sciences* (London: Routledge, 1988), pp. 31–48.

―― 'Variations on Variation – or Picasso back to Bach', in Nelson Goodman and Catherine Z. Elgin (eds), *Reconceptions in Philosophy and the Other Arts and Sciences* (London: Routledge, 1988), pp. 66–82.

Greenberg, Clement, 'Modernist Painting' reprinted in Alex Neill and Aaron Ridley (eds), *The Philosophy of Art: Readings Ancient and Modern* (New York: McGraw-Hill, 1995), pp. 111–17.

Guthrie, W. K. C., *The Greek Philosophers: From Thales to Aristotle* (London: Methuen, 1967).

Haldane, John, 'Higher Education After Ideology: Whose Crisis? What Knowledge?', in R. Barnett and A. Griffin (eds), *The End of Knowledge in Higher Education* (London: Cassell, 1997), pp. 53–66.

Jormakka, Kari, 'The Most Architectural Thing', in Thomas Mical (ed.), *Surrealism and Architecture* (London: Routledge, 2005), pp. 290–317.

Jorn, Asger, 'Architecture for Life', *Potlatch* 15 (22 December 1954).

Kant, Immanuel, *Critique of Judgement* (trans. Werner S. Pluhar; Indianapolis: Hackett, 1987).

Kierkegaard, Søren, *Fear and Trembling* (trans. Walter Lowrie; Princeton: Princeton University Press, 1945).

Larkin, Philip, 'Skin', in *The Less Deceived* (London: The Marvell Press, 1977).

Leach, Neil (ed.), *Rethinking Architecture: A Reader in Cultural Theory* (London: Routledge, 1997).

Lévi-Strauss, Claude, *The Raw and the Cooked* (trans. J. and D. Weightman; London, Jonathan Cape: 1969).

McGinn, Colin, *The Character of Mind* (Oxford: Oxford University Press, 1982).

―― *The Subjective View* (Oxford: Clarendon Press, 1983).

―― *Mental Content* (Oxford: Basil Blackwell, 1989).

Marshall, Peter, *Demanding the Impossible* (London: Fontana, 1992).

Matravers, Derek, *Art and Emotion* (Oxford: Clarendon Press, 1998).

Meager, Ruby, 'Seeing Paintings', *Proceedings of the Aristotelian Society*, Supplementary vol. 40 (1966), pp. 63–84.

Mical, Thomas (ed.), *Surrealism and Architecture* (London: Routledge, 2005).

O'Shaughnessy, Brian, *Consciousness and the World* (Oxford: Oxford University Press, 2000).

Podro, Michael, *The Critical Historians of Art* (London: Yale University Press, 1982).

Porphyrios, Demitri, 'Classicism is not a Style', in *Architectural Design* 5/6 (1982), pp. 50–57.

Putnam, Hilary, 'Brains in a Vat', in *Reason, Truth and History* (New York: Cambridge University Press, 1981), pp. 1–21.

Rabaté, Jean-Michel, 'Introduction 2003: Are You History?', in John Sturrock, *Structuralism* (Oxford: Basil Blackwell, 2003), pp. 1–16.

Saussure, Ferdinand de, *Course in General Linguistics* (trans. Roy Harris; London: Duckworth, 1983).

BIBLIOGRAPHY

Scruton, Roger, *The Aesthetics of Architecture* (London: Methuen, 1979).
——*The Classical Vernacular: Architectural Principles in an Age of Nihilism* (Manchester: Carcanet Press, 1994).
——*Modern Philosophy* (London: Sinclair-Stevenson, 1994).
——'Continental Philosophy from Fichte to Sartre', in Anthony Kenny (ed.), *The Oxford Illustrated History of Western Philosophy* (Oxford: Oxford University Press, 1994).
——*Be Attitudes, Poems and Libretti* (n.p.: The Garsdon Press, 1997).
Sim, Stuart, 'Structuralism and Post-structuralism', in *Philosophical Aesthetics: An Introduction* (ed. Oswald Hanfling; Oxford: Basil Blackwell, 1992), pp. 405–39.
Sturrock, John, *Structuralism* (Oxford: Basil Blackwell, 2003).
Summerson, John, *The Classical Language of Architecture* (Cambridge: MIT, 1987).
Szirtes, George, 'The Courtyards', from *The Photographer in Winter* (reprinted in George Szirtes, *Selected Poems 1976–1996*; Oxford: Oxford University Press, 1996).
Viollet-le-Duc, *Discourses on Architecture* (trans. B. Bucknell; London: Allen and Unwin, 1959).
Vitruvius, *The Ten Books of Architecture* (trans. M. Morgan; New York: Dover, 1960).
Winters, Edward, 'Aesthetic Appreciation', *The Journal of Aesthetic Education* 32 (July 1998), pp. 1–10.
——'Architecture', in Berys Gaut and Dominic McIver Lopes (eds), *The Routledge Companion to Aesthetics* (London: Routledge, 2nd edn, 2005), pp. 655–67.
Wittgenstein, Ludwig, *The Philosophical Investigations*, (trans. G. E. M. Anscombe; Oxford: Basil Blackwell, 1963).
——*Zettel* (eds, G. E. M. Anscombe and G. H. von Wright; trans. G. E. M. Anscombe; Oxford: Basil Blackwell, 2nd edn, 1967).
——*The Blue and Brown Books: Preliminary Studies for the 'Philosophical Investigations'*, (Oxford: Basil Blackwell, 2nd edn, 1969).
——*Philosophical Grammar* (ed. Rush Rhees; trans. Anthony Kenny; Oxford: Basil Blackwell, 1974).
——*Culture and Value* (ed. G. H. von Wright; trans. Peter Winch; Oxford: Basil Blackwell, 1980).
——*Remarks on the Philosophy of Psychology*, vol. II (eds, G. H. von Wright and H. Nyman; trans. C. G. Luckhardt and M. A. E. Aue; Oxford: Basil Blackwell, 1980).
Wollheim, Richard, *Painting As An Art* (London: Thames and Hudson, 1987).
——'On Pictorial Representation', in Rob van Gerwen (ed.), *Richard Wollheim on the Art of Painting: Art as Representation and Expression* (Cambridge University Press, 2001), pp. 13–27.

INDEX

Aiken, John 102
Alberti, Leon Battista 17
Alen, William van 55
Allington, Ed 102
allusion 19, 142–5
Alpher, David 89
Alsop, Will 103
Anscombe, G. E. M. 36
appreciation 2, 4, 5, 8, 9, 10, 16, 19, 20, 21, 24, 39, 40, 55, 73, 74, 87, 104, 110, 130, 132, 133, 137, 143, 145, 148, 153, 158, 162
Archigram 97
Aristotle 42–3, 118
Asplund, Erik Gunnar 153

Barthes, Roland 8, 68–9, 76, 89, 97
Bartok, Bela 89
Bauhaus 45–6
beauty 31, 41, 47, 99, 106, 136, 146, 161
  dependent (or fixed) 31, 32, 34, 38, 39, 54, 100, 101, 103
  free 32, 35, 38, 39–40, 101
Beethoven, Ludwig van 55
belief 20, 25, 30, 36, 53–4, 110–15, 116, 119, 128, 155
Berkeley, Bishop 25, 124
blindsight 129–30
Botton, Alain de 46
Brahms, Johannes 143
Breton, André 95
Bryson, Norman 70–5, 92, 110, 128–30

categorical imperative 26, 29, 30
Chambers, William 17
CIAM 45, 69
Clark, T. J. 96
classicism 5, 15–24, 50–2
classical orders 5, 15, 16, 19, 128
concepts 110, 112, 116, 122, 123
conceptual architecture 98
consciousness 20–1, 110–15, 117, 119, 133, 135
  false 7, 44–5, 97
contractualism 26–7
Coppola, Francis Ford 143
Corbusier, Le 9, 37

Dada 35–6
Debord, Guy 95, 96
denotation 84–5
derive 96, 97
Derrida, Jacques 76–83, 130, 132
Descartes, René 25
détournement 96
disposition 112, 153
Dogon people 92

Eco, Umberto 81–2
Eiffel Tower 8, 68
Eisenmann, Peter 82–3
Enlightenment 25, 26, 61
Exemplification 85
existentialism 9, 93–4, 95
Eyck, Aldo van 8, 69, 92
experience 8, 20–4, 30, 31, 88, 114,

INDEX

115, 120–1, 125, 127, 133, 135, 138, 162
aesthetic 6, 31, 53, 75, 100, 146
 imaginative 118–21, 130, 137–9, 144, 145, 151, 153
 expression 87, 140, 143–4

Fifty Cent 143
Florence, Penny 143
formalism 34–5, 97, 100
Forty, Adrian 41, 44, 77
frame 11, 146
Freud, Sigmund 61, 111, 135
functionalism 6–7, 37, 38–48, 50, 55, 56–7

genius 102
Goethe, Johann Wolfgang von 143
Goodman, Nelson 8, 9, 83, 84–90, 132–5, 137, 152, 156
Gormley, Antony 102
Goya, Francisco de 55, 140
Greenberg, Clement 32, 34–5, 100–1
Greene, David 97, 98
Gropius, Walter 45
Guthrie, W. K. C. 43
Guy, Mike 87, 88

Haldane, John 157–8
Hadid, Zaha 3, 103
Hart, Frederik 104
Hawksmoor, Nicholas 56
Hertzberger, Hermann 69
Holl, Steven 89
Hume, David 25
hypothetical imperative 28

imagination 26, 31, 110, 113, 117–20, 138, 151
inhabitation 10
intention 110, 111, 135
interpretation 89–91

Jacobsen, Arne 85, 86, 133
Jarray, Tess 102
Jorn, Asger 95, 96, 136, 147

Kant, Immanuel 1–2, 6, 25–6, 28–32, 38–9, 53, 100–3, 115, 120
'Kant's Prayer' 33
Kent, Tim 145, 146, 154
Kierkegaard, Søren 93–4, 98
knowledge 113, 115, 116

Leibniz, Gottfried Wilhelm 25
Lévi-Strauss, Claude 8, 66–7
Libeskind, Daniel 3, 103
literature 17
Locke, John 25, 124
Lomax, Tom 102

Mach, David 102
Marx, Karl 135
Marxism 94–6
Matravers, Derek 155
Meager, Ruby 155, 156
meaning 8, 16, 62–5, 71–5, 76–8, 88, 89, 121, 126, 127, 131, 145, 148
mental images 119, 122, 124
Meyer, Hannes 45–6
Mies van der Rohe, Ludwig 34–5
mimesis 5, 17, 50–1
modernism 3, 6–8, 24, 25–37, 41, 50, 52–5, 102
Mondrian, Piet 61
moral action 6
morality 26, 101, 104, 136
music 22, 34, 39, 55, 132, 143

Noriega, General Manuel 143

O'Shaughnessy, Brian 120

painting 17, 19, 20, 21, 32, 34, 38, 52, 55, 119, 128

INDEX

Peirce, Charles Sanders 8, 9, 84, 89, 132
perception 20–1, 25, 70, 110, 115–17, 118–21, 128, 129, 144, 162
 manifold of 25, 120
phenomenology 112, 114, 115, 119, 128, 129
Picasso, Pablo 32, 33, 89, 144
Plato 43
poetry 32–3
Porphyrios, Demitri 17
post-structuralism 8, 9, 76–83, 89, 130, 132
propositions 110, 112, 123
propositional attitudes 110–12, 114, 115, 135
Propp, Vladimir 66–7
public art 99–106, 137
Putnam, Hilary 124–5

Rawls, John 26
reason 28, 29–30
 aesthetic (or critical) 30, 53, 100
 practical 28, 29–30, 53, 100
 theoretical 53, 100
reference 84
 mediated 88
representation 17–20, 140–2
Rousseau, Jean-Jacques 26

St John Wilson, Colin 153
Sartre, Jean-Paul 33, 93, 94
Saussure, Ferdinand de 8, 9, 61–5, 70, 76, 93, 122, 124, 126, 130
Schelling, Freidrich Wilhelm Joseph 143
Scruton, Roger 42, 44, 148–51

sculpture 2–3, 17, 19, 20, 38–9
sensations 113, 114–15
sign 62–5, 70, 81, 92, 122, 129, 132
Sim, Stuart 65
Situationist International 9, 10, 95–7, 135–6
situationism 9
situationists 9, 10, 142
Spinoza, Benedict de 25
structuralism 8, 61–75, 89, 93, 122, 127, 130, 133
Sturrock, John 122
Summerson, John 165
Szirtes, George 156–7, 158, 159

Team X 69
Terry, Quinlan 5, 149
Till, Jeremy 161
Tschumi, Bernard 79–82, 96, 132

Utzon, Jørn 85, 133, 142

Vaneigem, Raoul 95, 96
Velàzquez, Diego de 145
Viollet-le-Duc 40–1
Vitruvius 5, 16, 17

Whiteread, Rachel 102
Wigglesworth, Sarah 161
Williams, Vaughan 22
Wilson, Richard 102
Wittgenstein, Ludwig 6, 23, 70–2, 91, 104, 110, 118, 120, 124, 128, 130, 153, 155, 156, 159
Wollheim, Richard 137–8

Ying Lin, Maya 104–6, 137, 140